JavaScript Made Easy: A Step-By-Step Guide

Anshuman Mishra

Published by Anshuman Mishra, 2025.

TITLE:
"JAVASCRIPT MADE EASY: A STEP-BY-STEP GUIDE "

CONTENT OUTLINE:

About the Book:

"JavaScript Made Easy: A Step-by-Step Guide for College Students" is designed specifically for college students who are new to programming or looking to enhance their JavaScript skills. The book takes a hands-on, step-by-step approach to learning JavaScript, breaking down complex concepts into simple, digestible sections. Each chapter builds on the previous one, ensuring that readers not only understand the syntax and logic of JavaScript but also develop a strong foundation in programming principles.

The book covers everything from basic syntax to advanced concepts like asynchronous programming, DOM manipulation, and using JavaScript in real-world web development. By the end of this book, readers will be equipped to build interactive, dynamic websites and web applications with confidence.

Key Features:

- **Clear, Step-by-Step Instructions**: Every concept is introduced in small, manageable chunks, making it easy to follow along and build on prior knowledge.
- **Hands-On Projects**: Practical examples and exercises at the end of each chapter will help solidify the learner's understanding.
- **Real-World Applications**: Focus on how JavaScript is used in real-world web development scenarios, including working with APIs and frameworks.
- **Student-Friendly**: Written specifically with the needs and learning pace of college students in mind, it includes easy-to-understand explanations, tips, and troubleshooting guides.

How to Study This Book:

1. **Start at the Beginning**:
   Don't rush through the chapters. Start with the basics, even if you have some prior knowledge. JavaScript can be tricky, and having a solid foundation is essential for understanding more complex concepts. Work through the introductory chapters and make sure you understand each concept before moving on.
2. **Follow the Examples**:
   This book contains numerous examples that illustrate JavaScript in action. As you read each section, try running the code examples in your browser or in an online JavaScript editor. Experiment by changing parts of the code and observing the results. This hands-on approach will help reinforce your understanding of the concepts.
3. **Complete the Exercises**:
   At the end of each chapter, there are exercises designed to help you apply what you've learned. Make sure to complete these exercises. They will help you practice and reinforce

the concepts discussed in the chapter. If you find an exercise difficult, don't skip it. Go back to the relevant section, review the content, and try again.

4. **Take It Step by Step**:
Each chapter builds upon the last, so don't jump ahead. If you're struggling with a particular concept, take the time to review it until you fully understand it. It's okay to take breaks and revisit previous chapters to refresh your knowledge.

5. **Work on the Final Project**:
The final project is a great way to bring everything you've learned together. It will challenge you to think critically about how to apply JavaScript in a practical scenario. Start planning your project early, and break it down into smaller tasks as you learn new concepts. This will give you a real sense of achievement when you complete it.

6. **Ask for Help**:
If you get stuck, don't hesitate to ask for help. Discuss concepts with classmates or seek assistance online in forums or communities dedicated to JavaScript. Understanding programming can be difficult at first, but persistent practice and collaboration will help you grow as a programmer.

7. **Review and Reinforce**:
Regularly review the chapters you've completed. Programming skills improve with consistent practice, and revisiting old material will help solidify your understanding. As you continue learning, you'll start to see how different concepts in JavaScript connect to each other, enhancing your overall comprehension.

8. **Build Projects Outside the Book**:
As you progress through the chapters, try applying what you've learned by building your own small projects. Creating simple applications, websites, or games is a fun way to practice and test your skills. The more you code, the more confident you will become in your abilities.

9. **Stay Curious**:
JavaScript is a powerful and versatile language with many features. While this book covers the essentials, don't be afraid to explore beyond it. Experiment with new libraries, frameworks, and tools once you've mastered the basics.

ABOUT THE AUTHOR:

ANSHUMAN KUMAR MISHRA IS A SEASONED EDUCATOR AND PROLIFIC AUTHOR WITH OVER 20 YEARS OF EXPERIENCE IN THE TEACHING FIELD. HE HAS A DEEP PASSION FOR TECHNOLOGY AND A STRONG COMMITMENT TO MAKING COMPLEX CONCEPTS ACCESSIBLE TO STUDENTS AT ALL LEVELS. WITH AN M.TECH IN COMPUTER SCIENCE FROM BIT MESRA, HE BRINGS BOTH ACADEMIC EXPERTISE AND PRACTICAL EXPERIENCE TO HIS WORK.

CURRENTLY SERVING AS AN ASSISTANT PROFESSOR AT DORANDA COLLEGE, ANSHUMAN HAS BEEN A GUIDING FORCE FOR MANY ASPIRING COMPUTER SCIENTISTS AND ENGINEERS, NURTURING THEIR SKILLS IN VARIOUS PROGRAMMING LANGUAGES AND TECHNOLOGIES. HIS TEACHING STYLE IS FOCUSED ON CLARITY, HANDS-ON LEARNING, AND MAKING STUDENTS COMFORTABLE WITH BOTH THEORETICAL AND PRACTICAL ASPECTS OF COMPUTER SCIENCE.

THROUGHOUT HIS CAREER, ANSHUMAN KUMAR MISHRA HAS AUTHORED OVER 25 BOOKS ON A WIDE RANGE OF TOPICS INCLUDING PYTHON, JAVA, C, C++, DATA SCIENCE, ARTIFICIAL INTELLIGENCE, SQL, .NET, WEB PROGRAMMING, DATA STRUCTURES, AND MORE. HIS BOOKS HAVE BEEN WELL-RECEIVED BY STUDENTS, PROFESSIONALS, AND INSTITUTIONS ALIKE FOR THEIR STRAIGHTFORWARD EXPLANATIONS, PRACTICAL EXERCISES, AND DEEP INSIGHTS INTO THE SUBJECTS.

ANSHUMAN'S APPROACH TO TEACHING AND WRITING IS ROOTED IN HIS BELIEF THAT LEARNING SHOULD BE ENGAGING, INTUITIVE, AND HIGHLY APPLICABLE TO REAL-WORLD SCENARIOS. HIS EXPERIENCE IN BOTH ACADEMIA AND INDUSTRY HAS GIVEN HIM A UNIQUE PERSPECTIVE ON HOW TO BEST PREPARE STUDENTS FOR THE EVOLVING WORLD OF TECHNOLOGY.

IN HIS BOOKS, ANSHUMAN AIMS NOT ONLY TO IMPART KNOWLEDGE BUT ALSO TO INSPIRE A LIFELONG LOVE FOR LEARNING AND EXPLORATION IN THE WORLD OF COMPUTER SCIENCE AND PROGRAMMING.

"JAVA Programming code should be written for developers to comprehend, and only incidentally for the compiler to execute."

— Anshuman Mishra

Copyright Page

Title: JavaScript Made Easy: A Step-by-Step Guide for College Students

Author: Anshuman Kumar Mishra
Copyright © 2025 by Anshuman Kumar Mishra

This book is published for educational purposes and is intended to serve as a comprehensive guide for MCA and BCA students, educators, and aspiring programmers. The author has made every effort to ensure accuracy, but neither the author nor the publisher assumes responsibility for errors, omissions, or any consequences arising from the application of information in this book.

CHAPTER-1

INTRODUCTION TO JAVASCRIPT

1. What is JavaScript?

JavaScript is a high-level, interpreted programming language that plays a crucial role in web development. Unlike HTML and CSS, which are used to structure and style web pages, JavaScript adds functionality and interactivity to websites. It is primarily used for front-end web development but also has powerful uses in back-end development when used with environments like **Node.js**.

Key Characteristics of JavaScript:

1. **High-Level Language**:
   As a high-level language, JavaScript abstracts away much of the complexity of machine-level operations. Developers can write code using simple syntax that is easy to read and write, without worrying about low-level memory management.
2. **Interpreted Language**:
   JavaScript is an interpreted language, meaning that it doesn't require a separate compilation step. The browser's JavaScript engine (like V8 in Chrome) reads and executes JavaScript code directly from the script. This makes it faster to run code and allows for immediate feedback when writing code.
3. **Dynamic and Interactive**:
   JavaScript allows you to create dynamic websites. This means that content can change on the fly based on user interaction, time, or other events, without needing to reload the entire page. Examples include pop-up messages, live form validation, real-time data updates, and interactive media.
4. **Event-Driven Programming**:
   JavaScript is commonly used in **event-driven programming**, meaning that it listens for events such as mouse clicks, key presses, form submissions, and more. Based on these events, JavaScript executes certain functions that change the behavior of the webpage.
5. **Runs on Client-Side**:
   JavaScript is traditionally run on the client-side (i.e., within the user's browser) rather than the server. This allows for faster interactions, as the browser can process JavaScript without having to wait for the server to respond.
6. **Versatile**:
   While JavaScript is most commonly used for web development, it is also used in server-side programming (via Node.js), mobile app development (via frameworks like React Native), desktop apps (via Electron), and game development.

Role in Web Development:

- **Interactivity**: JavaScript is used to make websites interactive. Without it, websites would be static, and all user interactions would require page reloads. Examples of interactivity include buttons, dropdown menus, sliders, form validation, and dynamic content updates.

- **Manipulating the DOM**: The **Document Object Model (DOM)** is an interface that represents the structure of an HTML document. JavaScript allows you to interact with the DOM to change, delete, or add elements to the page. This enables dynamic changes like updating content, changing styles, or creating new HTML elements based on user input.
- **AJAX (Asynchronous JavaScript and XML)**: JavaScript allows you to retrieve and send data to a server asynchronously without refreshing the page. This makes modern websites feel faster and smoother. It is widely used for tasks like fetching new content, submitting forms, or updating information without reloading the entire page.
- **Validation**: JavaScript is used to validate forms before they are submitted to the server. For example, checking if all required fields are filled out, if an email address is in the correct format, or if a password meets certain security criteria. This provides instant feedback to the user and reduces server load.
- **Control Multimedia**: JavaScript can control multimedia content such as audio and video. It can play, pause, seek, and adjust the volume of media files, enabling more advanced media players on websites.

Example: Basic JavaScript Program

Let's break down a simple example of JavaScript code and explain how it works within an HTML document:

HTML and JavaScript Example:

```
<!DOCTYPE html>
<html lang="en">
<head>
    <meta charset="UTF-8">
    <meta name="viewport" content="width=device-width, initial-scale=1.0">
    <title>JavaScript Example</title>
</head>
<body>
    <h1>Welcome to JavaScript!</h1>
    <script>
        // This is a simple JavaScript program
        alert("Hello, welcome to JavaScript!");
    </script>
</body>
</html>
```

Explanation of the Code:

1. **HTML Structure**:
   - The structure of the document is typical of any HTML page:
     - The `<head>` section includes metadata such as character encoding (`<meta charset="UTF-8">`) and viewport settings.
     - The `<body>` contains the visible content on the webpage, such as the heading `<h1>`.

2. **The `<script>` Tag**:
   o The `<script>` tag is where we place our JavaScript code inside an HTML document. This tag can be placed either in the `<head>` or `<body>` sections of the document, though it's often better to place it at the end of the `<body>` to ensure the page content loads before the script runs.
   o In this example, the JavaScript code inside the `<script>` tag will execute once the page loads.
3. **The `alert()` Function**:
   o Inside the `<script>` tag, the code calls the JavaScript function `alert("Hello, welcome to JavaScript!");`.
   o This function displays a pop-up dialog box with the text inside the parentheses, in this case, "Hello, welcome to JavaScript!".
   o **Note**: The `alert()` function is often used for debugging or providing simple messages to users. However, it's considered intrusive for user interfaces in production websites.
4. **How It Works**:
   o When the webpage is loaded in the browser, the browser reads the HTML code.
   o It encounters the `<script>` tag and executes the JavaScript inside it.
   o In this case, as soon as the page loads, the browser will pop up a small alert box displaying "Hello, welcome to JavaScript!".
   o The user must click "OK" to close the alert before they can interact with the webpage.

Practical Usage:

- While the `alert()` function is useful for demonstrating basic JavaScript functionality, it is rarely used in real-world applications for user interaction. Instead, JavaScript typically manipulates elements within the webpage (like showing or hiding content, changing the color of text, or dynamically loading new data) without interrupting the user experience.

How JavaScript Interacts with HTML and CSS:

- JavaScript is tightly integrated with both HTML and CSS:
   o **HTML** provides the structure of the web page (e.g., text, buttons, forms).
   o **CSS** controls the presentation of the page (e.g., colors, layout, fonts).
   o **JavaScript** brings the page to life by making it interactive. For example, JavaScript can change the content of HTML elements or adjust their style dynamically, allowing for more interactive experiences.

2. Setting Up the Development Environment

Before you begin writing JavaScript code, it's essential to set up a development environment that allows you to write, test, and debug your code. Fortunately, setting up a JavaScript development environment is straightforward and doesn't require complex tools or configurations.

Here's a detailed guide to setting up a simple yet effective development environment for JavaScript:

Basic Requirements for JavaScript Development

1. **Text Editor**:
   A text editor is where you'll write your JavaScript code. There are many choices available, but some of the most popular options include:
   - **VS Code (Visual Studio Code)**:
     This is the most popular and feature-rich editor for JavaScript. It provides syntax highlighting, IntelliSense (auto-completion), debugging tools, and extensions that make writing code more efficient.
       - Features include integrated Git support, terminal, code snippets, and extensions for linting, auto-formatting, and more.
   - **Sublime Text**:
     Sublime Text is lightweight, fast, and highly customizable. It's excellent for beginners or developers who prefer a minimal interface. It has support for plugins and extensions but lacks some of the advanced features found in VS Code.
   - **Atom**:
     Atom is an open-source text editor built by GitHub. It is customizable and offers various packages to extend its functionality. Like Sublime Text, it is lightweight but comes with a greater focus on collaboration and version control integration.
2. **Web Browser**:
   Since JavaScript is a client-side language, it runs directly in the browser. Therefore, you'll need a modern web browser to test your code. The most commonly used browsers for JavaScript development are:
   - **Google Chrome**:
     Known for its speed and developer-friendly tools, Chrome offers excellent debugging features via **Chrome DevTools**.
   - **Mozilla Firefox**:
     Firefox also offers robust developer tools and is known for its privacy and performance optimizations.
   - **Microsoft Edge**:
     Based on Chromium, Edge has become a strong option for web development, offering many similar features to Chrome.
   - **Safari**:
     The default browser for macOS, Safari provides the necessary developer tools for web development on Apple devices.
3. **(Optional) Local Server**:
   For more advanced JavaScript development, particularly when working with server-side JavaScript (e.g., Node.js) or APIs, you may need a local server. A local server allows you to run backend code or serve web pages dynamically.
   - **Live Server (VS Code Extension)**:
     This is a useful extension for Visual Studio Code that enables live-reloading for your HTML, CSS, and JavaScript files. When you save a file, it automatically updates the browser to reflect the changes, making it easier to develop in real time.
   - **XAMPP/WAMP**:
     These are local server environments that you can install on your computer. They

are especially useful for PHP, but they can also run JavaScript via Node.js. XAMPP is a cross-platform solution, while WAMP is specifically for Windows users.

Steps to Set Up Your JavaScript Development Environment

Step 1: Install a Text Editor

First, download and install your preferred text editor. **Visual Studio Code** is highly recommended because it's free, feature-rich, and widely used by JavaScript developers.

1. Visit the Visual Studio Code website.
2. Download the installer for your operating system (Windows, macOS, or Linux).
3. Follow the installation instructions to set up VS Code on your machine.

Step 2: Open Your Text Editor

Once your text editor is installed, open it. For this example, we'll assume you're using **VS Code**:

- Launch **Visual Studio Code** from your applications folder or start menu.

Step 3: Create Your First File

Now it's time to create your first file to test your JavaScript setup.

1. Open **VS Code**.
2. Create a new file by selecting **File > New File** or pressing Ctrl + N (Windows) or Cmd + N (Mac).
3. Save the file by choosing **File > Save As**, and name the file index.html.

In this index.html file, you'll write some basic HTML and include JavaScript inside a <script> tag.

Here's the example code you can use:

```
<!DOCTYPE html>
<html lang="en">
<head>
    <meta charset="UTF-8">
    <meta name="viewport" content="width=device-width, initial-scale=1.0">
    <title>JavaScript Setup Example</title>
</head>
<body>
```

```
    <h1>JavaScript Setup</h1>
    <script>
        console.log("JavaScript is working!");
    </script>
</body>
</html>
```

- **Explanation**:
    - o The HTML structure defines the basic layout for your webpage.
    - o Inside the `<script>` tag, JavaScript code is added. In this case, it simply outputs "JavaScript is working!" to the browser console.
    - o This is a basic example to verify that your setup is correct.

Step 4: Run Your Code

Now that you've written your HTML and JavaScript, it's time to run the file and see if everything works as expected.

1. Save the `index.html` file (press `Ctrl + S` or `Cmd + S`).
2. Open the `index.html` file in your web browser by double-clicking it or right-clicking it and choosing **Open with** > your preferred browser.

Step 5: Test in Browser Console

After opening the HTML file in a web browser, the JavaScript should execute. However, since we used `console.log()` in the JavaScript, you will not see a pop-up message on the page. Instead, you'll need to check the **browser console**.

1. In **Google Chrome**, right-click anywhere on the page and select **Inspect**. This opens the Developer Tools.
2. Switch to the **Console** tab.
3. If everything is set up correctly, you should see the message `"JavaScript is working!"` printed in the console.

This confirms that your JavaScript code is functioning properly and the development environment is set up correctly.

Example: Simple JavaScript Setup for Testing

To recap, here's a simple, complete HTML and JavaScript file that you can use to test your setup:

```
<!DOCTYPE html>
```

```
<html lang="en">
<head>
    <meta charset="UTF-8">
    <meta name="viewport" content="width=device-width, initial-scale=1.0">
    <title>JavaScript Setup Example</title>
</head>
<body>
    <h1>JavaScript Setup</h1>
    <script>
        console.log("JavaScript is working!");
    </script>
</body>
</html>
```

Summary of the Setup Process

1. **Install a Text Editor** (VS Code recommended) to write your JavaScript code.
2. **Create an HTML file** (e.g., `index.html`) and include JavaScript inside a `<script>` tag.
3. **Run the HTML file in your browser** to see the result and check the JavaScript output in the browser console.
4. **Use Developer Tools** in your browser (right-click > Inspect > Console) to view JavaScript logs and troubleshoot your code.

By following these steps, you'll have a simple yet powerful development environment for JavaScript set up in no time. You can then start exploring more complex JavaScript functionality, libraries, and frameworks as you progress in your learning journey.

3. Understanding the Role of JavaScript in Web Development

JavaScript is a core component of modern web development. It is often referred to as the "interactive" part of the web because it adds dynamic functionality to websites, allowing them to respond to user actions and update content without the need for page reloads. In the context of web development, HTML, CSS, and JavaScript work together to build a fully functional website:

- **HTML** (Hypertext Markup Language) provides the structure of the website.
- **CSS** (Cascading Style Sheets) handles the presentation and styling.
- **JavaScript** brings interactivity and dynamic behavior to the web page.

JavaScript is responsible for turning a static page into an engaging and interactive experience, and its role in web development can be broken down into several key areas:

Role of JavaScript in Web Development

1. Interactivity

JavaScript makes websites interactive by allowing them to respond to user actions like clicks, keyboard inputs, or mouse movements. This interactivity is essential for creating a smooth and engaging user experience.

Examples:

- **Form Validation:** Before submitting a form, JavaScript can check if the fields are filled out correctly (e.g., ensuring that an email address is in the correct format).
- **Event Handling:** JavaScript listens for events like clicks, hover, or key presses, allowing you to trigger actions based on user input.
- **Dynamic Updates Without Reloading:** JavaScript can dynamically update parts of the page (like adding items to a shopping cart) without needing to reload the entire page.

Example: Click Event

Here's an example of how JavaScript adds interactivity to a webpage by changing the text when a button is clicked:

```
<!DOCTYPE html>
<html lang="en">
<head>
    <meta charset="UTF-8">
    <meta name="viewport" content="width=device-width, initial-scale=1.0">
    <title>JavaScript Click Event</title>
</head>
<body>
    <h1 id="greeting">Hello!</h1>
    <button onclick="changeText()">Click Me</button>

    <script>
        function changeText() {
            document.getElementById("greeting").innerHTML = "You clicked the
button!";
        }
    </script>
</body>
</html>
```

Explanation:

- The button uses the `onclick` event to call the `changeText()` function when clicked.
- The function changes the content of the `<h1>` element with the id `greeting` to display the message "You clicked the button!".
- This is a simple but powerful example of how JavaScript can make a website interactive.

2. Dynamic Content

JavaScript allows you to manipulate the HTML and CSS of a page dynamically. You can change the content, styles, and structure of a page without the need to reload it. This is crucial for making websites more interactive and engaging.

Examples:

- **Changing the Style of Elements:** JavaScript can change the appearance of an element, such as altering its color, size, or position in response to user actions.
- **Modifying Content:** JavaScript can dynamically update the content on the page, such as displaying new information or updating a counter.

Example: Changing Style Dynamically

Here's an example where JavaScript changes the color of an element when a button is clicked:

```html
<!DOCTYPE html>
<html lang="en">
<head>
    <meta charset="UTF-8">
    <meta name="viewport" content="width=device-width, initial-scale=1.0">
    <title>JavaScript Dynamic Style</title>
</head>
<body>
    <h1 id="title">Click the button to change color!</h1>
    <button onclick="changeColor()">Change Color</button>

    <script>
        function changeColor() {
            document.getElementById("title").style.color = "red";
        }
    </script>
</body>
</html>
```

Explanation:

- The `changeColor()` function is triggered when the button is clicked.
- It targets the `<h1>` element with the id `title` and changes its `style.color` property to "red", dynamically altering the appearance of the text.

---

3. Asynchronous Operations

JavaScript supports asynchronous programming, meaning that it can perform tasks like loading data or making API requests without blocking the rest of the code. This allows for smoother and faster user experiences since the browser doesn't need to refresh the page to load new content.

Examples:

- **AJAX (Asynchronous JavaScript and XML)** and the `fetch()` API allow JavaScript to send requests to a server, retrieve data, and update the page without needing a page reload.
- This capability is often used for real-time updates, like loading new content on social media feeds or making live search suggestions.

Example: Fetching Data from an API

Here's an example of using the `fetch()` API to asynchronously fetch data from a server and display it on a webpage:

```html
<!DOCTYPE html>
<html lang="en">
<head>
    <meta charset="UTF-8">
    <meta name="viewport" content="width=device-width, initial-scale=1.0">
    <title>JavaScript Fetch API</title>
</head>
<body>
    <h1>Fetch API Example</h1>
    <button onclick="fetchData()">Get Data</button>
    <div id="result"></div>

    <script>
        function fetchData() {
            fetch('https://jsonplaceholder.typicode.com/posts/1')
                .then(response => response.json())
                .then(data => {
                    document.getElementById('result').innerHTML = data.title;
                })
                .catch(error => console.error('Error:', error));
        }
    </script>
</body>
</html>
```

Explanation:

- When the button is clicked, the `fetchData()` function is called.
- The `fetch()` function makes an HTTP request to an API and returns a promise.
- Once the data is fetched, the `.then()` method processes the response and updates the page without reloading it, displaying the title of the post in the `result` div.

---

4. Building Web Applications

JavaScript is also used to build full-fledged web applications, often in combination with libraries and frameworks like **React**, **Angular**, and **Vue.js**. These tools allow developers to create complex, data-driven websites and apps that respond to user interactions in real-time.

Examples:

- **Single-Page Applications (SPAs):** JavaScript frameworks like React enable the creation of SPAs, where the entire application is loaded once, and navigation between pages doesn't require a full page reload.
- **Real-Time Web Apps:** Applications like online chat services, collaborative editing, and live feeds rely heavily on JavaScript for real-time updates and interactivity.

Example: A Simple Web App Using JavaScript

A basic to-do list application is a good example of how JavaScript powers modern web apps. Users can add tasks, mark them as completed, and delete them, all without refreshing the page.

Here's a simple, conceptual overview of how such a web app would work:

- **HTML** provides the structure (the list of tasks).
- **CSS** styles the app to make it look visually appealing.
- **JavaScript** adds interactivity, like adding new tasks to the list, toggling their completion status, or deleting them.

In conclusion, **JavaScript** is an essential tool in web development, enabling interactivity, dynamic content, and seamless user experiences. By setting up a proper development environment and understanding the core concepts, you will be ready to begin building interactive websites and applications using JavaScript.

25 multiple-choice questions (MCQ

Topic 1: What is JavaScript?

1. **What is JavaScript primarily used for?**
   - a) Data storage
   - b) Creating dynamic and interactive web pages
   - c) Managing databases
   - d) Creating graphics and images

   Answer: b) Creating dynamic and interactive web pages
2. **Which of the following is NOT a feature of JavaScript?**
   - a) Event handling
   - b) Dynamic content update
   - c) Styling web pages
   - d) Form validation

   Answer: c) Styling web pages
3. **What type of language is JavaScript?**
   - a) Compiled
   - b) Interpreted

- o c) Machine language
- o d) Assembly language
  - **Answer:** b) Interpreted
4. **Where does JavaScript run in a web environment?**
   - o a) Server-side
   - o b) In the cloud
   - o c) Browser
   - o d) Operating system
     - **Answer:** c) Browser
5. **Which HTML tag is used to include JavaScript in a webpage?**
   - o a) `<javascript>`
   - o b) `<script>`
   - o c) `<js>`
   - o d) `<code>`
     - **Answer:** b) `<script>`
6. **Which method is used to show a message in a pop-up box in JavaScript?**
   - o a) `alert()`
   - o b) `console.log()`
   - o c) `show()`
   - o d) `messageBox()`
     - **Answer:** a) `alert()`
7. **Which of the following can JavaScript NOT do?**
   - o a) Validate user input
   - o b) Manipulate HTML and CSS
   - o c) Create responsive designs
   - o d) Connect to a server directly via the filesystem
     - **Answer:** d) Connect to a server directly via the filesystem
8. **How do you declare a variable in JavaScript?**
   - o a) `var x = 10;`
   - o b) `declare x = 10;`
   - o c) `variable x = 10;`
   - o d) `dim x = 10;`
     - **Answer:** a) `var x = 10;`
9. **Which of these is a valid JavaScript comment?**
   - o a) `<!-- This is a comment -->`
   - o b) `/* This is a comment */`
   - o c) `// This is a comment //`
   - o d) `# This is a comment`
     - **Answer:** b) `/* This is a comment */`
10. **What will this JavaScript code output?** `console.log(2 + 3 * 4);`
    - o a) 14
    - o b) 20
    - o c) 10
    - o d) 12
      - **Answer:** a) 14

Topic 2: Setting up the Development Environment

11. **Which of the following is a popular text editor for JavaScript development?**
    - o a) Microsoft Word
    - o b) Visual Studio Code
    - o c) Notepad
    - o d) Excel

    Answer: b) Visual Studio Code

12. **Which of the following is NOT necessary for setting up a basic JavaScript development environment?**
    - o a) A text editor
    - o b) A web browser
    - o c) A database
    - o d) A JavaScript runtime

    Answer: c) A database

13. **How do you run a JavaScript file in the browser?**
    - o a) By opening the `.js` file in the browser
    - o b) By including the `.js` file in an HTML document
    - o c) By typing the JavaScript code in the browser console
    - o d) By saving the file in the `c:/` drive

    Answer: b) By including the `.js` file in an HTML document

14. **Which of the following browsers is suitable for JavaScript development?**
    - o a) Internet Explorer
    - o b) Safari
    - o c) Google Chrome
    - o d) All of the above

    Answer: d) All of the above

15. **What is the purpose of the "Live Server" extension in Visual Studio Code?**
    - o a) To deploy code to the server
    - o b) To open a live chat session for support
    - o c) To reload the page automatically when code changes
    - o d) To test JavaScript on the server

    Answer: c) To reload the page automatically when code changes

16. **Which HTML file extension should be used when writing a JavaScript program in an HTML document?**
    - o a) `.txt`
    - o b) `.js`
    - o c) `.html`
    - o d) `.xml`

    Answer: c) `.html`

17. **Which JavaScript feature allows for real-time inspection of code while the page is loaded in the browser?**
    - o a) Browser console
    - o b) Inspect tool
    - o c) Developer tools

o d) All of the above
Answer: d) All of the above

18. **What is the first step in setting up a development environment for JavaScript?**
   o a) Installing Node.js
   o b) Installing a text editor
   o c) Writing JavaScript code
   o d) Configuring the server
   Answer: b) Installing a text editor

19. **What is the shortcut to open the developer console in most browsers?**
   o a) F12
   o b) Ctrl + Shift + I
   o c) Ctrl + P
   o d) Both a and b
   Answer: d) Both a and b

20. **What should you do after writing JavaScript in a file called `script.js` to include it in an HTML file?**
   o a) `<script src="script.js"></script>`
   o b) `<script file="script.js"></script>`
   o c) `<include src="script.js"></include>`
   o d) `<load src="script.js"></load>`
   Answer: a) `<script src="script.js"></script>`

Topic 3: Understanding the Role of JavaScript in Web Development

21. **JavaScript is primarily used to add which of the following features to web pages?**
   o a) Structure
   o b) Styling
   o c) Interactivity
   o d) Images
   Answer: c) Interactivity

22. **Which of the following is a common use of JavaScript in web development?**
   o a) Designing the layout
   o b) Validating user input
   o c) Organizing server data
   o d) Optimizing SEO
   Answer: b) Validating user input

23. **JavaScript can be used to perform which of the following tasks on a webpage?**
   o a) Change content dynamically
   o b) Control multimedia
   o c) Create animations
   o d) All of the above
   Answer: d) All of the above

24. **Which of these JavaScript features allows for real-time data updates on a webpage?**
   o a) Dynamic content manipulation
   o b) Asynchronous operations (AJAX, Fetch API)
   o c) Event handling

o d) Styling elements

Answer: b) Asynchronous operations (AJAX, Fetch API)

25. **What is the role of JavaScript in a Single Page Application (SPA)?**

o a) To handle only styling
o b) To manage server-side data
o c) To update the page dynamically without reloading
o d) To manage user authentication

Answer: c) To update the page dynamically without reloading

CHAPTER-2

BASICS OF JAVASCRIPT

1. Variables and Data Types

Variables in JavaScript are used to store data values. Once a variable is declared, it can be used to hold various types of data, such as numbers, strings, objects, or even functions. In JavaScript, you declare variables using one of three keywords: var, let, and const.

- **var** (Older Way):
    - Historically, var was the primary way to declare variables in JavaScript.
    - **Scope**: var is function-scoped, which means that if a variable is declared inside a function, it is accessible within that function and all nested functions. It is not block-scoped, which can cause unintended behavior in certain cases (e.g., inside loops or conditionals).
    - **Hoisting**: var declarations are hoisted to the top of their scope, meaning the variable is available throughout the function (or globally if declared outside any function), but its value will not be assigned until the line where it's initialized.

Example of var:

```
function exampleVar() {
    console.log(x);   // undefined, because `x` is hoisted but not yet
assigned
    var x = 10;
    console.log(x);   // 10, after initialization
}

exampleVar();
```

- **let** (Modern Way):
    - let is used to declare variables in modern JavaScript.
    - **Scope**: let is block-scoped, which means the variable is accessible only within the block (e.g., inside loops, conditionals, functions) where it is declared.
    - **Hoisting**: let is hoisted but doesn't initialize the variable until the line where it's declared (known as the "temporal dead zone"). Accessing the variable before its initialization results in a ReferenceError.

Example of let:

```
let name = "John";   // Declare a variable using let
console.log(name);    // Outputs: John

if (true) {
    let age = 25;     // `age` is only accessible inside this block
    console.log(age); // Outputs: 25
}
// console.log(age); // Error: age is not defined outside the block
```

- **const** (For Constants):
  - ○ const is used to declare variables whose values cannot be reassigned after initialization.
  - ○ **Scope**: const is also block-scoped, similar to let.
  - ○ **Immutability**: The value of a const variable cannot be changed. However, if the value is an object or array, its properties or elements can still be modified, as the reference to the object or array is constant.

Example of const:

```
const pi = 3.14159; // Declare a constant
console.log(pi);    // Outputs: 3.14159

// pi = 3.14; // Error: Assignment to constant variable.

const person = { name: "Alice", age: 25 };
person.age = 26;  // Allowed: modifying properties of the object
console.log(person.age);  // Outputs: 26
```

2. Data Types in JavaScript:

JavaScript supports two main types of data: **Primitive data types** and **Reference data types**.

Primitive Data Types (Immutable):

Primitive data types are the simplest types of data. They are immutable, meaning their values cannot be changed after they are created.

1. **String**:
   - ○ Represents a sequence of characters (text).
   - ○ Strings can be enclosed in either single quotes ('), double quotes ("), or backticks (`) for template literals.

Example:

```
let name = "John";      // String using double quotes
let greeting = 'Hello'; // String using single quotes
let sentence = `My name is ${name}.`; // String using backticks for
template literals
console.log(sentence);  // Outputs: My name is John.
```

2. **Number**:
   - ○ Represents both integers and floating-point numbers.
   - ○ JavaScript does not distinguish between integer and floating-point numbers. They are both of type number.

Example:

```
let age = 25;          // Integer
let price = 99.99;     // Floating-point number
```

```
let result = age + price;
console.log(result);    // Outputs: 124.99
```

3. **Boolean**:
   - o Represents a value of either `true` or `false`.
   - o Useful in conditions, loops, and logical operations.

   Example:

```
let isActive = true;    // Boolean value
let isCompleted = false;
console.log(isActive);  // Outputs: true
console.log(isCompleted); // Outputs: false
```

4. **Null**:
   - o Represents the absence of a value or a non-existent object.
   - o `null` is intentionally set to indicate that a variable does not have any value.

   Example:

```
let value = null; // No value assigned to this variable
console.log(value);  // Outputs: null
```

5. **Undefined**:
   - o A variable is `undefined` if it has been declared but not assigned a value.
   - o It is also the default value of a function argument if no value is provided.

   Example:

```
let x;  // Variable declared but not assigned a value
console.log(x);  // Outputs: undefined
```

6. **Symbol** (ES6):
   - o Represents a unique and immutable identifier. Symbols are often used as unique property keys for objects.

   Example:

```
let uniqueSymbol = Symbol('description');
let obj = {
    [uniqueSymbol]: "This is a unique symbol property"
};
console.log(obj[uniqueSymbol]);  // Outputs: This is a unique symbol
property
```

Reference Data Types (Mutable):

Reference data types are more complex and can be modified after creation.

1. **Object**:

- An object is a collection of key-value pairs. Objects are useful for storing and organizing related data.

Example:

```
let person = {
    name: "Alice",
    age: 25,
    greet: function() {
        console.log("Hello, " + this.name);
    }
};
person.greet(); // Outputs: Hello, Alice
```

2. **Array**:
   - An array is an ordered list of values. Arrays can store multiple values of different data types.

Example:

```
let colors = ["Red", "Green", "Blue"];
console.log(colors[0]); // Outputs: Red
colors.push("Yellow");  // Adds "Yellow" to the array
console.log(colors);    // Outputs: ["Red", "Green", "Blue", "Yellow"]
```

3. **Function**:
   - A function is a block of code designed to perform a specific task. Functions can accept inputs (parameters) and return outputs (results).

Example:

```
function add(a, b) {
    return a + b;
}
let sum = add(5, 10);  // Function call
console.log(sum);       // Outputs: 15
```

3. Example of Declaring Variables with Different Data Types:

```
let str = "Hello, World!";  // String
let num = 42;               // Number
let isActive = true;        // Boolean
let emptyValue = null;      // Null
let notDefined;             // Undefined

let person = {              // Object
    name: "Alice",
    age: 25
};

let colors = ["Red", "Green", "Blue"]; // Array

function greet() {          // Function
    console.log("Hello!");
```

```
}
greet();  // Calls the greet function, outputs: Hello!
```

2. Operators and Expressions

Operators in JavaScript:

Operators in JavaScript are used to perform operations on variables and values. They can manipulate data, compare values, assign values to variables, or perform logical operations. JavaScript has several categories of operators:

1.1. Arithmetic Operators:

Arithmetic operators are used to perform basic mathematical operations. They include addition, subtraction, multiplication, division, modulo, and increment/decrement.

- **+ (Addition)**: Adds two operands.
- **− (Subtraction)**: Subtracts the second operand from the first.
- *** (Multiplication)**: Multiplies two operands.
- **/ (Division)**: Divides the first operand by the second.
- **% (Modulo)**: Returns the remainder of the division.
- **++ (Increment)**: Increases the value of a variable by 1.
- **−− (Decrement)**: Decreases the value of a variable by 1.

Example:

```
let a = 5;
let b = 2;

console.log(a + b);   // 7 (addition)
console.log(a - b);   // 3 (subtraction)
console.log(a * b);   // 10 (multiplication)
console.log(a / b);   // 2.5 (division)
console.log(a % b);   // 1 (modulo)
console.log(a++);     // 5 (increment, outputs 5, then a becomes 6)
console.log(--a);     // 5 (decrement, a becomes 5, then outputs 5)
```
1.2. Assignment Operators:

Assignment operators are used to assign values to variables. They allow you to store values in variables in different ways:

- **=**: Assigns the right-hand value to the left-hand variable.
- **+=**: Adds the right-hand value to the left-hand variable and assigns the result to the left-hand variable.
- **−=**: Subtracts the right-hand value from the left-hand variable and assigns the result to the left-hand variable.
- ***=**: Multiplies the left-hand variable by the right-hand value and assigns the result to the left-hand variable.

- **/=:** Divides the left-hand variable by the right-hand value and assigns the result to the left-hand variable.

Example:

```
let x = 10;
x += 5;   // x = x + 5 => 15
x -= 3;   // x = x - 3 => 12
console.log(x);   // Outputs: 12

x *= 2;   // x = x * 2 => 24
x /= 4;   // x = x / 4 => 6
console.log(x);   // Outputs: 6
```

1.3. Comparison Operators:

Comparison operators are used to compare two values. These operators return a boolean value (`true` or `false`) based on the comparison.

- **==:** Equal to (loose equality) – compares values, but not types.
- **===:** Strictly equal to – compares both value and type.
- **!=:** Not equal to – checks if two values are not equal.
- **>:** Greater than.
- **<:** Less than.
- **>=:** Greater than or equal to.
- **<=:** Less than or equal to.

Example:

```
let a = 10;
let b = 5;

console.log(a > b);      // true (10 is greater than 5)
console.log(a === 10);   // true (a is strictly equal to 10)
console.log(b != 5);     // false (b is equal to 5)
console.log(a <= 20);    // true (a is less than or equal to 20)
```

1.4. Logical Operators:

Logical operators are used to combine or invert boolean values. These operators are crucial in control flow and decision-making processes.

- **&& (Logical AND):** Returns `true` if both operands are `true`.
- **|| (Logical OR):** Returns `true` if at least one of the operands is `true`.
- **! (Logical NOT):** Reverses the logical state of its operand. If the operand is `true`, it becomes `false`, and vice versa.

Example:

```
let x = true;
let y = false;
```

```
console.log(x && y);   // false (both must be true, but y is false)
console.log(x || y);   // true (at least one must be true, x is true)
console.log(!x);       // false (negates x, which is true)
```
1.5. Ternary Operator:

The ternary operator is a shorthand for an `if-else` statement. It evaluates a condition and returns one of two expressions based on whether the condition is `true` or `false`.

- **Syntax**: `condition ? expression1 : expression2`

Example:

```
let age = 20;
let result = (age >= 18) ? "Adult" : "Minor";
console.log(result);   // Outputs: Adult
```
2. Expressions in JavaScript:

An expression is any valid unit of code that resolves to a value. It can be a single value, a variable, or a combination of values, operators, and variables. Expressions can be classified into simple and complex expressions.

2.1. Simple Expression:

A simple expression is a single value or variable that directly evaluates to a value.

- **Example**:

```
5              // A simple expression that evaluates to 5
let x = 3;     // A variable, which is an expression that evaluates to 3
```
2.2. Complex Expression:

A complex expression is a combination of values, variables, and operators that evaluates to a value. Complex expressions can be mathematical, logical, or even function calls.

- **Example**:

```
 (x + y) * z - 10    // A complex expression involving addition,
multiplication, and subtraction
```

Practical Example of Expressions:

```
let x = 5;
let y = 10;
let z = 2;

let result = (x + y) * z - 10; // Complex expression
console.log(result);   // Outputs: 20 ((5 + 10) * 2 - 10 = 20)
```

Operators in JavaScript:

Operators in JavaScript are used to perform operations on variables and values. They can manipulate data, compare values, assign values to variables, or perform logical operations. JavaScript has several categories of operators:

1.1. Arithmetic Operators:

Arithmetic operators are used to perform basic mathematical operations. They include addition, subtraction, multiplication, division, modulo, and increment/decrement.

- **+ (Addition)**: Adds two operands.
- **– (Subtraction)**: Subtracts the second operand from the first.
- *** (Multiplication)**: Multiplies two operands.
- **/ (Division)**: Divides the first operand by the second.
- **% (Modulo)**: Returns the remainder of the division.
- **++ (Increment)**: Increases the value of a variable by 1.
- **-- (Decrement)**: Decreases the value of a variable by 1.

Example:

```
let a = 5;
let b = 2;

console.log(a + b);    // 7 (addition)
console.log(a - b);    // 3 (subtraction)
console.log(a * b);    // 10 (multiplication)
console.log(a / b);    // 2.5 (division)
console.log(a % b);    // 1 (modulo)
console.log(a++);      // 5 (increment, outputs 5, then a becomes 6)
console.log(--a);      // 5 (decrement, a becomes 5, then outputs 5)
```

1.2. Assignment Operators:

Assignment operators are used to assign values to variables. They allow you to store values in variables in different ways:

- **=**: Assigns the right-hand value to the left-hand variable.
- **+=**: Adds the right-hand value to the left-hand variable and assigns the result to the left-hand variable.
- **–=**: Subtracts the right-hand value from the left-hand variable and assigns the result to the left-hand variable.
- ***=**: Multiplies the left-hand variable by the right-hand value and assigns the result to the left-hand variable.
- **/=**: Divides the left-hand variable by the right-hand value and assigns the result to the left-hand variable.

Example:

```
let x = 10;
x += 5;   // x = x + 5 => 15
x -= 3;   // x = x - 3 => 12
console.log(x);   // Outputs: 12

x *= 2;   // x = x * 2 => 24
x /= 4;   // x = x / 4 => 6
console.log(x);   // Outputs: 6
```

1.3. Comparison Operators:

Comparison operators are used to compare two values. These operators return a boolean value (`true` or `false`) based on the comparison.

- `==`: Equal to (loose equality) – compares values, but not types.
- `===`: Strictly equal to – compares both value and type.
- `!=`: Not equal to – checks if two values are not equal.
- `>`: Greater than.
- `<`: Less than.
- `>=`: Greater than or equal to.
- `<=`: Less than or equal to.

Example:

```
let a = 10;
let b = 5;

console.log(a > b);     // true (10 is greater than 5)
console.log(a === 10); // true (a is strictly equal to 10)
console.log(b != 5);   // false (b is equal to 5)
console.log(a <= 20);  // true (a is less than or equal to 20)
```

1.4. Logical Operators:

Logical operators are used to combine or invert boolean values. These operators are crucial in control flow and decision-making processes.

- `&&` **(Logical AND)**: Returns `true` if both operands are `true`.
- `||` **(Logical OR)**: Returns `true` if at least one of the operands is `true`.
- `!` **(Logical NOT)**: Reverses the logical state of its operand. If the operand is `true`, it becomes `false`, and vice versa.

Example:

```
let x = true;
let y = false;

console.log(x && y);   // false (both must be true, but y is false)
console.log(x || y);   // true (at least one must be true, x is true)
console.log(!x);       // false (negates x, which is true)
```

1.5. Ternary Operator:

The ternary operator is a shorthand for an `if-else` statement. It evaluates a condition and returns one of two expressions based on whether the condition is `true` or `false`.

- **Syntax:** `condition ? expression1 : expression2`

Example:

```
let age = 20;
let result = (age >= 18) ? "Adult" : "Minor";
console.log(result);   // Outputs: Adult
```

2. Expressions in JavaScript:

An expression is any valid unit of code that resolves to a value. It can be a single value, a variable, or a combination of values, operators, and variables. Expressions can be classified into simple and complex expressions.

2.1. Simple Expression:

A simple expression is a single value or variable that directly evaluates to a value.

- **Example:**

```
5               // A simple expression that evaluates to 5
let x = 3;      // A variable, which is an expression that evaluates to 3
```

2.2. Complex Expression:

A complex expression is a combination of values, variables, and operators that evaluates to a value. Complex expressions can be mathematical, logical, or even function calls.

- **Example:**

```
 (x + y) * z - 10    // A complex expression involving addition,
multiplication, and subtraction
```

Practical Example of Expressions:

```
let x = 5;
let y = 10;
let z = 2;

let result = (x + y) * z - 10; // Complex expression
console.log(result);   // Outputs: 20 ((5 + 10) * 2 - 10 = 20)
```

3. Functions and Scope

A function is a reusable block of code designed to perform a specific task. Functions allow us to organize code efficiently and avoid repetition. Functions can accept input values (parameters) and return output (return value). They are fundamental for structuring and organizing complex programs.

1.1. Function Declaration:

A function is typically declared using the `function` keyword, followed by the function name, parameters (optional), and a block of code enclosed in curly braces `{}`.

- **Syntax:**

```
function functionName(parameter1, parameter2) {
    // code to execute
}
```

Example:

```
function greet(name) {
    console.log("Hello, " + name + "!");
}

greet("John");  // Outputs: Hello, John!
greet("Alice"); // Outputs: Hello, Alice!
```

In this example:

- The function `greet` takes a parameter `name`.
- It outputs a greeting message to the console.
- The function is called twice with different arguments ("John" and "Alice").

1.2. Return Statement:

Functions can return a value using the `return` keyword. When the function reaches a `return` statement, it stops executing, and the value after the `return` keyword is sent back to the caller.

- **Syntax:**

```
function functionName(parameter1, parameter2) {
    return result;  // Returns the result to the caller
}
```

Example:

```
function add(a, b) {
    return a + b;  // Returns the sum of a and b
}
```

```
let sum = add(10, 5);
console.log(sum);   // Outputs: 15
```

In this example:

- The add function takes two parameters a and b.
- It returns their sum.
- The result is stored in the variable sum, and the sum is logged to the console.

---

2. Scope in JavaScript:

Scope in JavaScript refers to the context in which variables are accessible. It determines where variables and functions can be used and modified in a program. There are different types of scope in JavaScript, including global scope, local scope, block scope, and lexical scope.

2.1. Global Scope:

A variable declared outside of any function or block is in the **global scope**. Variables in the global scope are accessible anywhere in the code, including inside functions.

- **Example:**

```
let globalVar = "I'm global!";   // Declared globally

function showGlobal() {
    console.log(globalVar);   // Accessible here
}

showGlobal();   // Outputs: I'm global!
console.log(globalVar);   // Outputs: I'm global!
```

In this example:

- The variable globalVar is declared in the global scope, so it can be accessed inside the function showGlobal() as well as outside of it.

2.2. Local Scope (Function Scope):

A variable declared inside a function is in **local scope** (or function scope). This means the variable is only accessible within that function, and trying to access it outside the function will result in an error.

- **Example:**

```
function myFunction() {
    let localVar = "I'm local!";   // Declared locally
    console.log(localVar);   // Accessible inside the function
```

```
}
myFunction();   // Outputs: I'm local!
console.log(localVar);   // Error: localVar is not defined
```

In this example:

- The variable `localVar` is declared inside the function `myFunction()`, so it can only be accessed within that function.
- Trying to access `localVar` outside the function results in an error because it's not defined in the global scope.

2.3. Block Scope:

In JavaScript, variables declared using `let` and `const` are **block-scoped**. This means they are only accessible within the block (usually a pair of curly braces `{}`) in which they are declared, such as inside an `if` statement, loop, or function.

- **Example:**

```
if (true) {
    let blockVar = "I'm block scoped!";   // Declared within the block
    console.log(blockVar);   // Accessible inside the block
}

console.log(blockVar);   // Error: blockVar is not defined
```

In this example:

- The variable `blockVar` is declared inside an `if` block using `let`, so it is only accessible within the `if` block.
- Attempting to access it outside the block results in an error because it is block-scoped.

2.4. Lexical Scope:

JavaScript follows **lexical scoping**, meaning that a function can access variables from its outer (enclosing) scope. This happens even if the function is called outside the scope in which it was declared. The scope is determined at the time the function is written, not when it's executed.

- **Example:**

```
function outerFunction() {
    let outerVar = "I am outside!";   // Declared in the outer function

    function innerFunction() {
        console.log(outerVar);   // Can access outerVar due to lexical scoping
    }

    innerFunction();   // Outputs: I am outside!
}
```

```
outerFunction();
```

In this example:

- The variable `outerVar` is declared in the outer function `outerFunction()`.
- The `innerFunction()` is able to access `outerVar` because of lexical scoping, even though `innerFunction()` is called inside `outerFunction()`.

Lexical scoping allows inner functions to remember and access variables from their outer environment, even after the outer function has finished executing.

Summary

- **Variables and Data Types**: Variables store values of different types like numbers, strings, and objects. Use `let`, `const`, and `var` to declare variables.
- **Operators and Expressions**: Operators perform operations on variables. Expressions combine values and operators to produce results.
- **Functions and Scope**: Functions encapsulate reusable code. Scope determines where variables can be accessed (global, local, block).

These concepts are fundamental to JavaScript programming, and understanding them is key to building dynamic web applications.

25 practical questions and answers based on the topics: **Variables and Data Types, Operators and Expressions**, and **Functions and Scope**.

Variables and Data Types

1. **Question:** How do you declare a string variable in JavaScript?
   - **Answer:**

   ```
   let greeting = "Hello, World!";
   console.log(greeting);  // Outputs: Hello, World!
   ```

2. **Question:** What is the difference between `null` and `undefined` in JavaScript?
   - **Answer:**

   ```
   let person = null;  // Explicitly assigned 'null'
   let city;  // 'undefined' by default as it is declared but not
   assigned
   console.log(person);  // Outputs: null
   ```

```
console.log(city);      // Outputs: undefined
```

3. **Question:** How do you declare and initialize a number variable in JavaScript?
   - **Answer:**

```
let age = 25;
let temperature = 22.5;
console.log(age);          // Outputs: 25
console.log(temperature); // Outputs: 22.5
```

4. **Question:** What is the result of this operation: `5 + "10"` in JavaScript?
   - **Answer:**

```
console.log(5 + "10");   // Outputs: "510" (string concatenation)
```

5. **Question:** How can you work with arrays in JavaScript?
   - **Answer:**

```
let fruits = ["Apple", "Banana", "Cherry"];
console.log(fruits[1]);   // Outputs: Banana
```

6. **Question:** How do you create and access an object in JavaScript?
   - **Answer:**

```
let user = { name: "Alice", age: 30 };
console.log(user.name);   // Outputs: Alice
```

7. **Question:** What is a `Symbol` in JavaScript, and how does it work?
   - **Answer:**

```
let sym1 = Symbol("id");
let sym2 = Symbol("id");
console.log(sym1 === sym2);   // Outputs: false (Symbols are
always unique)
```

8. **Question:** How do you handle mixed data types in an array in JavaScript?
   - **Answer:**

```
let mixedArray = [25, "John", true, {city: "New York"}, null];
console.log(mixedArray[3].city);   // Outputs: New York
```

Operators and Expressions

9. **Question:** How do you add two numbers in JavaScript using arithmetic operators?
   - **Answer:**

```
let x = 5;
let y = 10;
```

```
let sum = x + y;
console.log(sum);   // Outputs: 15
```

10. **Question:** What does the `%` operator do in JavaScript?
    o **Answer:**

```
let a = 15;
let b = 4;
let remainder = a % b;
console.log(remainder);   // Outputs: 3 (remainder of division)
```

11. **Question:** How do you subtract and assign the result to a variable in JavaScript?
    o **Answer:**

```
let z = 20;
z -= 5;   // Same as z = z - 5
console.log(z);   // Outputs: 15
```

12. **Question:** What does the `===` operator check in JavaScript?
    o **Answer:**

```
let num1 = 5;
let num2 = "5";
console.log(num1 === num2);   // Outputs: false (strict equality,
type matters)
```

13. **Question:** How does the `&&` operator work in JavaScript?
    o **Answer:**

```
let isAdult = true;
let hasTicket = false;
console.log(isAdult && hasTicket);   // Outputs: false (both must
be true)
```

14. **Question:** How do you negate a boolean value in JavaScript?
    o **Answer:**

```
let isActive = true;
console.log(!isActive);   // Outputs: false (inverts the boolean)
```

15. **Question:** What is the syntax for a ternary operator in JavaScript?
    o **Answer:**

```
let age = 18;
let status = (age >= 18) ? "Adult" : "Minor";
console.log(status);   // Outputs: Adult
```

16. **Question:** How do you increment and decrement a variable in JavaScript?

- o **Answer:**

```
let count = 5;
count++;
console.log(count);   // Outputs: 6 (increment by 1)
count--;
console.log(count);   // Outputs: 5 (decrement by 1)
```

17. **Question:** How do you combine multiple expressions in JavaScript?
    - o **Answer:**

```
let a = 10;
let b = 20;
let result = (a + b) * 2;
console.log(result);   // Outputs: 60 (first add a and b, then
multiply by 2)
```

18. **Question:** How do you concatenate strings in JavaScript?
    - o **Answer:**

```
let firstName = "John";
let lastName = "Doe";
let fullName = firstName + " " + lastName;
console.log(fullName);   // Outputs: John Doe
```

Functions and Scope

19. **Question:** How do you define a function that returns a value in JavaScript?
    - o **Answer:**

```
function multiply(a, b) {
    return a * b;
}
let result = multiply(3, 4);
console.log(result);   // Outputs: 12
```

20. **Question:** What happens if you try to access a local variable outside its function scope?
    - o **Answer:**

```
function displayInfo() {
    let name = "Alice";   // Local variable
    console.log(name);
}
displayInfo();   // Outputs: Alice
// console.log(name);   // Error: name is not defined outside the
function
```

21. **Question:** How do you access both global and local variables in JavaScript?

- o **Answer:**

```
let globalVar = "I am global";  // Global variable

function display() {
    let localVar = "I am local";  // Local variable
    console.log(globalVar);  // Accessible
    console.log(localVar);    // Accessible
}
display();  // Outputs: I am global, I am local
```

22. **Question:** How can you set default values for function parameters in JavaScript?
    - o **Answer:**

```
function greet(name = "Guest") {
    console.log("Hello, " + name + "!");
}
greet();            // Outputs: Hello, Guest!
greet("Alice");     // Outputs: Hello, Alice!
```

23. **Question:** How do arrow functions work in JavaScript?
    - o **Answer:**

```
const add = (x, y) => x + y;
console.log(add(5, 3));  // Outputs: 8
```

24. **Question:** What is block scope in JavaScript, and how do you use it with `let`?
    - o **Answer:**

```
if (true) {
    let blockScopedVar = "Inside block";
    console.log(blockScopedVar);  // Outputs: Inside block
}
// console.log(blockScopedVar);  // Error: blockScopedVar is not
defined outside the block
```

25. **Question:** How does lexical scoping work in JavaScript?
    - o **Answer:**

```
function outer() {
    let outerVar = "I'm from outer!";

    function inner() {
        console.log(outerVar);  // Inner function can access
outerVar due to lexical scoping
    }

    inner();  // Outputs: I'm from outer!
}

outer();
```

25 multiple-choice questions (MCQs) based on the topics: **Variables and Data Types**, **Operators and Expressions**, and **Functions and Scope**

Variables and Data Types

1. **Which of the following is the correct syntax to declare a variable in JavaScript?**
   - a) `var = myVar;`
   - b) `let myVar;`
   - c) `declare myVar;`
   - d) `variable myVar;`
   - **Answer:** b) `let myVar;`

2. **What will the following code output?**

```
let x = "Hello";
let y = "World";
console.log(x + y);
```

   - a) `Hello World`
   - b) `HelloWorld`
   - c) `WorldHello`
   - d) Error
   - **Answer:** a) `Hello World`

3. **Which data type is used to represent true or false values in JavaScript?**
   - a) String
   - b) Number
   - c) Boolean
   - d) Object
   - **Answer:** c) Boolean

4. **What will be the value of `typeof null` in JavaScript?**
   - a) `object`
   - b) `null`
   - c) `undefined`
   - d) `boolean`
   - **Answer:** a) `object`

5. **Which of the following is used to create an array in JavaScript?**
   - a) `[]`
   - b) `{}`
   - c) `()`
   - d) `<>`
   - **Answer:** a) `[]`

6. **Which of the following is NOT a primitive data type in JavaScript?**
   - a) String
   - b) Number
   - c) Boolean

- o d) Array
- o **Answer:** d) Array

7. **What will the following code output?**

```
let person = { name: "Alice", age: 25 };
console.log(person.name);
```

- o a) `undefined`
- o b) `"Alice"`
- o c) `25`
- o d) `null`
- o **Answer:** b) `"Alice"`

8. **Which of the following is the correct way to create a Symbol in JavaScript?**
- o a) `let sym = Symbol();`
- o b) `let sym = new Symbol();`
- o c) `let sym = createSymbol();`
- o d) `let sym = Symbol.create();`
- o **Answer:** a) `let sym = Symbol();`

9. **What is the result of `typeof []` in JavaScript?**
- o a) `array`
- o b) `object`
- o c) `undefined`
- o d) `null`
- o **Answer:** b) `object`

10. **Which of the following can hold different data types in JavaScript?**
- o a) String
- o b) Number
- o c) Array
- o d) Boolean
- o **Answer:** c) Array

Operators and Expressions

11. **What is the result of `10 % 3` in JavaScript?**
- o a) 3
- o b) 1
- o c) 10
- o d) 0
- o **Answer:** b) 1

12. **Which of the following operators is used for strict equality in JavaScript?**
- o a) `==`
- o b) `=`
- o c) `===`
- o d) `!=`

- o **Answer:** c) ===
13. **What is the result of `5 + "10"` in JavaScript?**
    - o a) `510`
    - o b) `15`
    - o c) `5 10`
    - o d) `NaN`
    - o **Answer:** a) `510`
14. **Which operator is used to combine multiple boolean expressions in JavaScript?**
    - o a) `||` (OR)
    - o b) `&&` (AND)
    - o c) `!` (NOT)
    - o d) `==` (Equal)
    - o **Answer:** b) `&&` (AND)
15. **What does the ++ operator do in JavaScript?**
    - o a) Decrements a variable
    - o b) Increments a variable
    - o c) Multiplies a variable
    - o d) Divides a variable
    - o **Answer:** b) Increments a variable
16. **What will be the value of `x` after the following code is executed?**

    ```
    let x = 10;
    x += 5;
    ```

    - o a) `15`
    - o b) `5`
    - o c) `10`
    - o d) `NaN`
    - o **Answer:** a) `15`
17. **What does the `!` operator do in JavaScript?**
    - o a) Negates a boolean value
    - o b) Assigns a value
    - o c) Compares two values
    - o d) Increments a value
    - o **Answer:** a) Negates a boolean value
18. **Which of the following is a valid way to perform a ternary operation in JavaScript?**
    - o a) `condition ? expr1 : expr2;`
    - o b) `if condition then expr1 else expr2;`
    - o c) `condition : expr1, expr2;`
    - o d) `if (condition) { expr1 } else { expr2 }`
    - o **Answer:** a) `condition ? expr1 : expr2;`
19. **What is the result of `10 / 2 * 5` in JavaScript?**
    - o a) `25`
    - o b) `20`
    - o c) `5`
    - o d) `NaN`

o **Answer:** b) `20`

20. **Which operator would you use to check inequality in JavaScript?**
    o a) `!=`
    o b) `==`
    o c) `===`
    o d) `>`
    o **Answer:** a) `!=`

Functions and Scope

21. **What is the correct syntax to declare a function in JavaScript?**
    o a) `function myFunction[]`
    o b) `function myFunction()`
    o c) `function:myFunction()`
    o d) `function myFunction[]{}`
    o **Answer:** b) `function myFunction()`

22. **What will be the output of the following code?**

```
function greet(name) {
    return "Hello, " + name;
}
console.log(greet("Alice"));
```

    o a) `Hello, Alice`
    o b) `Alice`
    o c) `Hello`
    o d) `undefined`
    o **Answer:** a) `Hello, Alice`

23. **What is the scope of a variable declared with `let` inside a function?**
    o a) Global scope
    o b) Local to the function
    o c) Block scope
    o d) Both local and global scope
    o **Answer:** b) Local to the function

24. **What is the result of trying to access a local variable outside the function in JavaScript?**
    o a) The variable is accessible
    o b) The variable returns `undefined`
    o c) An error occurs
    o d) The value is `null`
    o **Answer:** c) An error occurs

25. What will the following code output?

```
let x = 10;
function outer() {
    let y = 20;
    function inner() {
        console.log(x, y);
    }
    inner();
}
outer();
```

- o a) 10 20
- o b) undefined 20
- o c) undefined undefined
- o d) Error
- o **Answer:** a) 10 20

CHAPTER-3

CONTROL FLOW AND LOGIC

Conditional Statements (if, else, switch)

Conditional statements are essential for controlling the flow of execution in a program. They allow you to make decisions based on specific conditions. In JavaScript, the common conditional statements are `if`, `else`, `else if`, and `switch`. These help in deciding which block of code should run depending on whether a given condition is true or false.

1. if Statement

The `if` statement allows you to execute a block of code if a specified condition evaluates to `true`. If the condition is `false`, the code inside the block is skipped.

Syntax:

```
if (condition) {
    // block of code
}
```

- `condition`: This is the expression that will be evaluated. If it resolves to `true`, the code inside the block is executed.

Example:

```
let age = 18;

if (age >= 18) {
    console.log("You are an adult.");
}
```

- **Explanation**:
  - The condition `age >= 18` is evaluated. If `true`, it prints `"You are an adult."`.
  - Since `age` is 18, the condition is true, and the message is logged.

Output:

```
You are an adult.
```

If the condition were `age = 16`, nothing would happen since no `else` block is present.

2. else Statement

The `else` statement is used to specify a block of code that will execute when the condition in the `if` statement is `false`.

Syntax:

```
if (condition) {
    // block of code if condition is true
} else {
    // block of code if condition is false
}
```

- If the `condition` is `false`, the code inside the `else` block is executed.

Example:

```
let age = 16;

if (age >= 18) {
    console.log("You are an adult.");
} else {
    console.log("You are a minor.");
}
```

- **Explanation**:
  - The condition `age >= 18` evaluates to `false`, so the code inside the `else` block runs.
  - Since `age` is 16, it prints `"You are a minor."`.

Output:

```
You are a minor.
```

3. else if Statement

The `else if` statement allows you to test multiple conditions. If the first condition in the `if` statement is `false`, the `else if` conditions are evaluated one by one.

Syntax:

```
if (condition1) {
    // block of code if condition1 is true
} else if (condition2) {
    // block of code if condition2 is true
} else {
    // block of code if all conditions are false
}
```

- You can chain multiple `else if` statements to handle multiple conditions.

Example:

```
let age = 22;
```

```
if (age < 18) {
    console.log("You are a minor.");
} else if (age >= 18 && age <= 21) {
    console.log("You are a young adult.");
} else {
    console.log("You are an adult.");
}
```

- **Explanation**:
  - First, it checks if `age < 18`, which is `false`.
  - Then, it checks `age >= 18 && age <= 21`, which is also `false`.
  - Finally, since none of the previous conditions were true, the code inside the `else` block is executed, printing `"You are an adult."`.

Output:

```
You are an adult.
```

4. switch Statement

The `switch` statement is an alternative to multiple `if-else` statements when you need to compare one variable to several possible values. It is more readable and often used when there are many possible options to check for.

Syntax:

```
switch (expression) {
    case value1:
        // block of code if expression == value1
        break;
    case value2:
        // block of code if expression == value2
        break;
    case value3:
        // block of code if expression == value3
        break;
    default:
        // block of code if no match is found
}
```

- `expression`: This is the value or expression to be compared against.
- `case value`: Each `case` compares the `expression` with the specified value. If they match, the code block runs.
- `break`: Stops the execution of the `switch` statement once a match is found.
- `default`: If none of the cases match, the `default` block is executed (optional).

Example:

```
let day = 2;
let dayName;
```

```
switch (day) {
    case 1:
        dayName = "Monday";
        break;
    case 2:
        dayName = "Tuesday";
        break;
    case 3:
        dayName = "Wednesday";
        break;
    default:
        dayName = "Unknown";
}

console.log(dayName); // Outputs: Tuesday
```

- **Explanation**:
    - The `switch` statement evaluates `day`. Since `day` is 2, it matches `case 2`, and assigns `"Tuesday"` to `dayName`.
    - The `break` statement ensures that the program exits the `switch` once the case has been executed.

Output:

```
Tuesday
```

Key Differences Between if-else and switch

- **if-else**:
    - Used when the condition is based on complex expressions or comparisons.
    - More flexible than `switch` for handling different types of conditions.
    - Suitable when the conditions involve ranges (e.g., checking if a number is greater than, less than, or equal to a value).
- **switch**:
    - Best suited for comparing a single value to multiple possible matches.
    - Makes the code more readable when dealing with multiple options.
    - Faster and more efficient for handling many comparisons of a single value.

When to Use Each Conditional Statement

- **Use if when:**
    - You need to check more complex conditions or multiple logical expressions.
- **Use else if when:**
    - You need to evaluate multiple conditions sequentially.
- **Use switch when:**
    - You need to check a single variable against many possible values (like days of the week or menu options).

Loops (for, while, do-while)

Loops are used to repeat a block of code multiple times until a specific condition is met. JavaScript provides three main types of loops: `for`, `while`, and `do-while`. Each loop is useful for different situations based on how you need to iterate through data or repeat a block of code.

1. for Loop

The `for` loop is typically used when you know in advance how many times you want to repeat a block of code. This loop consists of three parts:

- **Initialization**: Defines and initializes the loop counter (or variable).
- **Condition**: A condition that is checked before every iteration. If it's `true`, the loop continues.
- **Increment/Decrement**: Updates the loop counter after each iteration.

Syntax:

```
for (initialization; condition; increment/decrement) {
    // block of code
}
```

Example:

```
or (let i = 1; i <= 5; i++) {
    console.log(i);
}
```

- **Explanation**:
  - **Initialization**: `let i = 1` — The counter `i` starts at 1.
  - **Condition**: `i <= 5` — The loop runs as long as `i` is less than or equal to 5.
  - **Increment**: `i++` — After each iteration, the value of `i` is incremented by 1.

Output:

```
1
2
3
4
5
```

2. while Loop

The `while` loop is used when you want to repeat a block of code as long as a condition is true. The condition is evaluated before each iteration, so the loop may not run at all if the condition is `false` initially.

Syntax:

```
while (condition) {
    // block of code
}
```

Example:

```
let i = 1;
while (i <= 5) {
    console.log(i);
    i++;
}
```

- **Explanation**:
    - The loop runs as long as i is less than or equal to 5.
    - Inside the loop, the value of i is printed, and then i is incremented manually with i++.

Output:

```
Copy code
1
2
3
4
5
```

3. do-while Loop

The do-while loop is similar to the while loop, but with a key difference: it executes the block of code **at least once** before checking the condition. This is because the condition is evaluated after the block of code runs.

Syntax:

```
do {
    // block of code
} while (condition);
```

Example:

```
let i = 1;
do {
    console.log(i);
    i++;
} while (i <= 5);
```

- **Explanation**:
    - The loop runs as long as i is less than or equal to 5.

- The block of code inside the `do` section runs first before the condition `i <= 5` is checked.

Output:

```
1
2
3
4
5
```

Since the condition is checked after the first execution, the loop runs at least once, even if the condition is false initially.

Comparison of Loops

- **for Loop**: Best when the number of iterations is known ahead of time. It is more compact since all the components (initialization, condition, increment) are in a single line.
- **while Loop**: Best when you need to repeat a block of code as long as a condition is true, but the number of iterations is not determined in advance.
- **do-while Loop**: Useful when you need to ensure that a block of code is executed at least once before checking the condition.

Summary with Practical Examples

Let's look at each type of loop with a simple practical example:

1. if-else Example:

This simple example uses an `if-else` statement to check whether the temperature is above or below 25 degrees.

```
let temperature = 30;
if (temperature > 25) {
    console.log("It's hot outside.");
} else {
    console.log("It's not too hot outside.");
}
```

Output:

```
It's hot outside.
```

2. switch Example:

This example shows how to use a `switch` statement to print a message based on the value of a `fruit` variable.

```
let fruit = "apple";
```

```
switch (fruit) {
    case "apple":
        console.log("It's an apple.");
        break;
    case "banana":
        console.log("It's a banana.");
        break;
    default:
        console.log("Unknown fruit.");
}
```

Output:

```
It's an apple.
```

3. for Loop Example:

This `for` loop prints the iteration number from 1 to 3.

```
for (let i = 1; i <= 3; i++) {
    console.log("Iteration number: " + i);
}
```

Output:

```
Iteration number: 1
Iteration number: 2
Iteration number: 3
```

4. while Loop Example:

This `while` loop prints the value of `counter` from 0 to 2.

```
let counter = 0;
while (counter < 3) {
    console.log("Counter value: " + counter);
    counter++;
}
```

Output:

```
Counter value: 0
Counter value: 1
Counter value: 2
```

5. do-while Loop Example:

This `do-while` loop will also print the counter value from 0 to 2, but since the condition is checked after the first run, it will always execute at least once.

```
let counter = 0;
do {
    console.log("Counter value: " + counter);
    counter++;
```

```
} while (counter < 3);
```

Output:

```
Counter value: 0
Counter value: 1
Counter value: 2
```

20 practical questions and answers covering Conditional Statements (if, else, switch) **and** Loops (for, while, do-while)

1. What will the following code print?

```
let num = 10;
if (num > 5) {
    console.log("Greater");
} else {
    console.log("Lesser");
}
```

Answer:
It will print `Greater` because 10 is greater than 5.

2. What is the output of the following code?

```
let score = 45;
if (score >= 50) {
    console.log("Pass");
} else {
    console.log("Fail");
}
```

Answer:
It will print `Fail` because the score is less than 50.

3. What will this code output?

```
let x = 7;
let y = "7";
if (x == y) {
    console.log("Equal");
} else {
    console.log("Not equal");
}
```

Answer:

It will print Equal because == only checks for value equality, not type equality.

---

4. What will the following code print?

```
let temperature = 30;
if (temperature < 25) {
    console.log("Cool");
} else if (temperature >= 25 && temperature <= 35) {
    console.log("Warm");
} else {
    console.log("Hot");
}
```

Answer:

It will print Warm because 30 is between 25 and 35.

---

5. What is the output of the following code?

```
let day = 2;
let dayName;

switch (day) {
    case 1:
        dayName = "Monday";
        break;
    case 2:
        dayName = "Tuesday";
        break;
    case 3:
        dayName = "Wednesday";
        break;
    default:
        dayName = "Unknown";
}

console.log(dayName);
```

Answer:

It will print Tuesday because day is 2.

---

6. What will the following code print?

```
let age = 18;
switch (true) {
```

```
    case (age < 18):
        console.log("Minor");
        break;
    case (age >= 18 && age < 60):
        console.log("Adult");
        break;
    case (age >= 60):
        console.log("Senior");
        break;
    default:
        console.log("Unknown age group");
}
```

Answer:
It will print `Adult` because the age is between 18 and 60.

7. What will the following code output?

```
let fruit = "apple";
switch (fruit) {
    case "apple":
        console.log("It's an apple");
        break;
    case "banana":
        console.log("It's a banana");
        break;
    default:
        console.log("Unknown fruit");
}
```

Answer:
It will print `It's an apple` because `fruit` is "apple".

8. What will be the output of the following code?

```
let x = 10;
if (x > 5 && x < 15) {
    console.log("Between 5 and 15");
} else {
    console.log("Out of range");
}
```

Answer:
It will print `Between 5 and 15` because 10 is within that range.

9. What will the following code print?

```
let age = 15;
if (age >= 18) {
    console.log("Adult");
} else {
    console.log("Minor");
}
```

Answer:
It will print `Minor` because 15 is less than 18.

10. What is the output of this code?

```
let number = 50;
if (number % 2 == 0) {
    console.log("Even");
} else {
    console.log("Odd");
}
```

Answer:
It will print `Even` because 50 is divisible by 2.

11. What will the following `for` loop print?

```
for (let i = 1; i <= 3; i++) {
    console.log("Iteration: " + i);
}
```

Answer:
It will print:

```
Iteration: 1
Iteration: 2
Iteration: 3
```

12. What is the output of the following `while` loop?

```
let i = 0;
while (i < 3) {
    console.log(i);
    i++;
```

```
}
```

Answer:
It will print:

```
0
1
2
```

---

13. What will the following do-while loop output?

```
let i = 3;
do {
    console.log(i);
    i++;
} while (i < 3);
```

Answer:
It will print:

```
Copy code
3
```

The loop runs at least once even though the condition is false after the first execution.

---

14. What is the output of the following for loop?

```
for (let i = 3; i > 0; i--) {
    console.log(i);
}
```

Answer:
It will print:

```
3
2
1
```

---

15. What will the following code print?

```
let counter = 0;
do {
    console.log("Counter: " + counter);
    counter++;
} while (counter < 2);
```

Answer:
It will print:

```
Counter: 0
Counter: 1
```

16. What will be the output of this `for` loop?

```
for (let i = 0; i <= 5; i++) {
    if (i === 3) {
        break;
    }
    console.log(i);
}
```

Answer:
It will print:

```
Copy code
0
1
2
```

The loop will stop execution when `i` equals 3 because of the `break` statement.

17. What will the following code print?

```
let x = 5;
while (x < 10) {
    console.log(x);
    x++;
}
```

Answer:
It will print:

```
5
6
7
8
9
```

18. What is the output of the following code?

```
let sum = 0;
```

```
for (let i = 1; i <= 5; i++) {
    sum += i;
}
console.log(sum);
```

Answer:
It will print 15, as the loop sums the numbers from 1 to 5.

---

19. What will the following code print?

```
let x = 3;
switch (x) {
    case 1:
        console.log("One");
        break;
    case 2:
        console.log("Two");
        break;
    default:
        console.log("Other");
}
```

Answer:
It will print Other because there is no case for x being 3.

---

20. What will be the output of this code?

```
let i = 1;
do {
    if (i === 3) {
        continue;
    }
    console.log(i);
    i++;
} while (i <= 5);
```

Answer:
It will print:

1
2
4
5

Since i === 3, the loop will skip printing 3 because of the continue statement.

25 multiple-choice questions (MCQs) on Conditional Statements (if, else, switch) and Loops (for, while, do-while)

Conditional Statements (if, else, switch)

1. What will be the output of the following code?

```
let number = 8;
if (number % 2 === 0) {
    console.log("Even");
} else {
    console.log("Odd");
}
```

- A) Even
- B) Odd
- C) Error
- D) Undefined

Answer: A) Even

2. What will the following code print?

```
let age = 20;
if (age > 18) {
    console.log("Adult");
} else {
    console.log("Minor");
}
```

- A) Minor
- B) Adult
- C) Error
- D) Undefined

Answer: B) Adult

3. In a switch statement, what happens if there is no matching `case`?

- A) It will throw an error
- B) The `default` case will be executed if present
- C) Nothing will happen

- D) It will break the program

Answer: B) The `default` case will be executed if present

---

4. Which of the following comparisons in the if statement would be correct for strict equality?

```
let num = "10";
if (num === 10) {
    console.log("True");
} else {
    console.log("False");
}
```

- A) True
- B) False
- C) Error
- D) Undefined

Answer: B) False

---

5. What is the output of the following code?

```
let day = 3;
switch (day) {
    case 1:
        console.log("Monday");
        break;
    case 3:
        console.log("Wednesday");
        break;
    default:
        console.log("Unknown Day");
}
```

- A) Monday
- B) Wednesday
- C) Unknown Day
- D) Error

Answer: B) Wednesday

---

6. What will the following code print?

```
let num = 20;
if (num > 10) {
    if (num < 30) {
        console.log("Between 10 and 30");
    }
} else {
    console.log("Less than 10");
}
```

- A) Between 10 and 30
- B) Less than 10
- C) Error
- D) Undefined

Answer: A) Between 10 and 30

---

7. What is the output of this code?

```
let color = "red";
if (color === "blue") {
    console.log("Blue");
} else if (color === "green") {
    console.log("Green");
} else {
    console.log("Other");
}
```

- A) Blue
- B) Green
- C) Other
- D) Error

Answer: C) Other

---

8. What will the following code output?

```
let x = 7;
if (x < 10) {
    console.log("Less than 10");
} else {
    console.log("Greater than or equal to 10");
}
```

- A) Less than 10

- B) Greater than or equal to 10
- C) Error
- D) Undefined

Answer: A) Less than 10

---

9. What will this code output?

```
let x = "10";
if (x == 10) {
    console.log("Equal");
} else {
    console.log("Not Equal");
}
```

- A) Equal
- B) Not Equal
- C) Error
- D) Undefined

Answer: A) Equal

---

10. What will be the output of the following switch statement?

```
let num = 5;
switch (num) {
    case 1:
        console.log("One");
        break;
    case 5:
        console.log("Five");
        break;
    default:
        console.log("Other");
}
```

- A) One
- B) Five
- C) Other
- D) Error

Answer: B) Five

Loops (for, while, do-while)

11. How many times will the following `for` loop run?

```
for (let i = 0; i < 5; i++) {
    console.log(i);
}
```

- A) 4 times
- B) 5 times
- C) 6 times
- D) Infinite

Answer: B) 5 times

---

12. What will the following `while` loop output?

```
let i = 1;
while (i < 4) {
    console.log(i);
    i++;
}
```

- A) 1 2 3
- B) 1 2 3 4
- C) Infinite loop
- D) 0 1 2

Answer: A) 1 2 3

---

13. How many iterations will this `do-while` loop run?

```
let count = 5;
do {
    console.log(count);
    count++;
} while (count < 5);
```

- A) 0
- B) 1
- C) 5
- D) Infinite

Answer: B) 1

14. What will the following `for` loop print?

```
for (let i = 1; i <= 3; i++) {
    if (i === 2) {
        continue;
    }
    console.log(i);
}
```

- A) 1 2 3
- B) 1 3
- C) 2 3
- D) Infinite

Answer: B) 1 3

15. What is the output of the following `while` loop?

```
let num = 0;
while (num < 5) {
    console.log(num);
    num++;
}
```

- A) 1 2 3 4 5
- B) 0 1 2 3 4
- C) Infinite loop
- D) 0

Answer: B) 0 1 2 3 4

16. What will the following code print?

```
let counter = 1;
do {
    console.log(counter);
    counter++;
} while (counter <= 3);
```

- A) 1 2 3
- B) 0 1 2 3
- C) 1 2
- D) 0 1 2

Answer: A) 1 2 3

---

17. What will be the output of this `for` loop?

```
for (let i = 5; i > 0; i--) {
    console.log(i);
}
```

- A) 5 4 3 2 1
- B) 1 2 3 4 5
- C) 5 4 3 2
- D) Infinite loop

Answer: A) 5 4 3 2 1

---

18. What is the output of the following `do-while` loop?

```
let num = 0;
do {
    console.log(num);
    num++;
} while (num < 3);
```

- A) 0 1 2 3
- B) 0 1 2
- C) 1 2 3
- D) 0

Answer: B) 0 1 2

---

19. How many times will this `for` loop run?

```
for (let i = 0; i < 10; i += 2) {
    console.log(i);
}
```

- A) 4 times
- B) 5 times
- C) 10 times
- D) Infinite

Answer: B) 5 times

20. What will be printed by the following code?

```
let i = 1;
while (i < 5) {
    if (i === 3) break;
    console.log(i);
    i++;
}
```

- A) 1 2
- B) 1 2 3
- C) 1 2 3 4
- D) Infinite

Answer: A) 1 2

21. What will be the output of this code?

```
let sum = 0;
for (let i = 1; i <= 3; i++) {
    sum += i;
}
console.log(sum);
```

- A) 3
- B) 6
- C) 1
- D) 0

Answer: B) 6

22. What will this code output?

```
let counter = 0;
for (let i = 0; i < 3; i++) {
    counter++;
}
console.log(counter);
```

- A) 1
- B) 2
- C) 3
- D) 0

Answer: C) 3

---

23. What will be the output of the following `while` loop?

```
let i = 1;
while (i < 10) {
    if (i === 5) {
        i++;
        continue;
    }
    console.log(i);
    i++;
}
```

- A) 1 2 3 4 6 7 8 9
- B) 1 2 3 4 5 6 7 8 9
- C) 1 2 3 4 5
- D) 5 6 7 8 9

Answer: A) 1 2 3 4 6 7 8 9

---

24. What will the following `for` loop print?

```
for (let i = 10; i >= 5; i--) {
    console.log(i);
}
```

- A) 10 9 8 7 6 5
- B) 5 6 7 8 9 10
- C) 1 2 3 4 5
- D) 5 4 3 2 1

Answer: A) 10 9 8 7 6 5

---

25. What is the output of the following `do-while` loop?

```
let i = 0;
do {
    if (i === 4) break;
    console.log(i);
    i++;
} while (i < 5);
```

- A) 0 1 2 3 4
- B) 0 1 2 3
- C) 1 2 3 4
- D) Infinite

Answer: B) 0 1 2 3

CHAPTER-4

WORKING WITH ARRAYS AND OBJECTS

Introduction to Arrays in JavaScript

An **array** in JavaScript is a special type of variable used to store multiple values in a **single variable**. Instead of creating separate variables for each value (e.g., `fruit1`, `fruit2`, etc.), arrays allow you to group these values together under a single variable name. Arrays can store a collection of different types of data such as **numbers, strings, objects,** or even other **arrays**.

Creating Arrays

In JavaScript, there are two primary ways to create an array:

1. Using Square Brackets [ ]

This is the most common and recommended way to create an array. The elements inside the array are separated by commas and enclosed in square brackets.

```
let fruits = ["Apple", "Banana", "Orange"];
```

In this example:

- `fruits` is the array variable.
- `"Apple"`, `"Banana"`, and `"Orange"` are the **elements** of the array.

The array `fruits` now contains 3 elements:

- Element at index 0: `"Apple"`
- Element at index 1: `"Banana"`
- Element at index 2: `"Orange"`

2. Using the Array Constructor

You can also create an array using the `Array` constructor. This approach is less commonly used, but it's useful when creating arrays dynamically.

```
let numbers = new Array(1, 2, 3, 4, 5);
```

Here:

- `numbers` is the array created using the `Array` constructor.
- The `new Array()` syntax creates an array with the specified elements: 1, 2, 3, 4, 5.

Note: You can also use the constructor with a single number to create an array of a certain length:

```
let emptyArray = new Array(5); // Creates an array with 5 empty slots
```

Accessing Array Elements

Each element in an array is stored at a specific **index**. Arrays in JavaScript are **zero-indexed**, which means that the first element is at index 0, the second element is at index 1, and so on.

Example:

```
let fruits = ["Apple", "Banana", "Orange"];
console.log(fruits[0]); // Outputs: Apple
console.log(fruits[1]); // Outputs: Banana
```

In the example above:

- `fruits[0]` accesses the first element of the `fruits` array, which is `"Apple"`.
- `fruits[1]` accesses the second element, which is `"Banana"`.

If you try to access an index that does not exist, like `fruits[10]`, you will get `undefined` because that index is out of range.

Array Length

The **length** property of an array tells you how many elements are in the array. It is a **dynamic** property, meaning that if you add or remove elements, the length will update automatically.

Example:
```
let fruits = ["Apple", "Banana", "Orange"];
console.log(fruits.length); // Outputs: 3
```

In the example above:

- `fruits.length` gives you the number of elements in the `fruits` array, which is 3.

This is useful when you want to perform tasks such as looping through all elements of an array or checking if the array has any elements.

Arrays Can Store Different Data Types

One important feature of JavaScript arrays is that they can store elements of different types. You can mix strings, numbers, objects, and even other arrays within the same array.

Example:
```
let mixedArray = [1, "Apple", true, { name: "John" }, [1, 2, 3]];
```

```
console.log(mixedArray[0]); // Outputs: 1
console.log(mixedArray[1]); // Outputs: Apple
console.log(mixedArray[3].name); // Outputs: John
console.log(mixedArray[4][1]); // Outputs: 2
```

- `mixedArray[0]` is a number: 1.
- `mixedArray[1]` is a string: "Apple".
- `mixedArray[3]` is an object, so `mixedArray[3].name` accesses the `name` property and outputs "John".
- `mixedArray[4]` is an array, so `mixedArray[4][1]` accesses the second element (2) of that inner array.

This flexibility allows arrays to be very versatile for storing different kinds of data together.

Array Methods and Operations

JavaScript provides a variety of built-in methods for manipulating arrays, allowing you to perform operations like adding, removing, and modifying elements. Below is an explanation of the most commonly used array methods, along with practical examples.

1. push()

- **Purpose:** Adds one or more elements to the end of an array and returns the new length of the array.
- **Syntax:** `array.push(element1, element2, ..., elementN)`

Example:
```
let fruits = ["Apple", "Banana"];
fruits.push("Orange"); // Adds "Orange" to the end of the array
console.log(fruits); // Outputs: ["Apple", "Banana", "Orange"]
```

- After using `push()`, the array `fruits` now contains three elements: "Apple", "Banana", and "Orange".

2. pop()

- **Purpose:** Removes the last element from an array and returns it.
- **Syntax:** `array.pop()`

Example:
```
let fruits = ["Apple", "Banana", "Orange"];
let lastFruit = fruits.pop(); // Removes "Orange"
console.log(fruits); // Outputs: ["Apple", "Banana"]
```

```
console.log(lastFruit); // Outputs: "Orange"
```

- After using `pop()`, the last element `"Orange"` is removed from the array and stored in `lastFruit`.

---

3. shift()

- **Purpose:** Removes the first element from an array and returns it.
- **Syntax:** `array.shift()`

Example:
```
let fruits = ["Apple", "Banana", "Orange"];
let firstFruit = fruits.shift(); // Removes "Apple"
console.log(fruits); // Outputs: ["Banana", "Orange"]
console.log(firstFruit); // Outputs: "Apple"
```

- The first element `"Apple"` is removed from the array, and the remaining elements are shifted to the left.

---

4. unshift()

- **Purpose:** Adds one or more elements to the beginning of an array and returns the new length of the array.
- **Syntax:** `array.unshift(element1, element2, ..., elementN)`

Example:
```
let fruits = ["Banana", "Orange"];
fruits.unshift("Apple"); // Adds "Apple" to the beginning
console.log(fruits); // Outputs: ["Apple", "Banana", "Orange"]
```

- After using `unshift()`, `"Apple"` is added to the beginning of the `fruits` array.

---

5. slice()

- **Purpose:** Returns a shallow copy of a portion of an array into a new array without modifying the original array.
- **Syntax:** `array.slice(startIndex, endIndex)`

Example:
```
let fruits = ["Apple", "Banana", "Orange", "Mango"];
let slicedFruits = fruits.slice(1, 3); // Returns a new array with index 1
and 2
console.log(slicedFruits); // Outputs: ["Banana", "Orange"]
console.log(fruits); // Outputs: ["Apple", "Banana", "Orange", "Mango"]
```

- The `slice()` method does not alter the original `fruits` array; it returns a new array with elements starting from index 1 up to (but not including) index 3.

6. splice()

- **Purpose:** Changes the contents of an array by removing or replacing existing elements and/or adding new elements.
- **Syntax:** `array.splice(startIndex, deleteCount, item1, item2, ...)`

Example:
```
let fruits = ["Apple", "Banana", "Orange"];
fruits.splice(1, 1, "Mango", "Grapes"); // Removes 1 element from index 1 and
adds "Mango" and "Grapes"
console.log(fruits); // Outputs: ["Apple", "Mango", "Grapes", "Orange"]
```

- The `splice()` method removes "Banana" and adds "Mango" and "Grapes" at index 1. This method directly modifies the original array.

7. forEach()

- **Purpose:** Executes a provided function once for each array element.
- **Syntax:** `array.forEach(callback)`

Example:
```
let fruits = ["Apple", "Banana", "Orange"];
fruits.forEach(function(fruit) {
    console.log(fruit);
});
// Outputs:
// Apple
// Banana
// Orange
```

- The `forEach()` method loops through each element of the `fruits` array and executes the provided function on each element.

8. map()

- **Purpose:** Creates a new array populated with the results of calling a provided function on every element in the calling array.
- **Syntax:** `array.map(callback)`

Example:
```
let numbers = [1, 2, 3, 4];
let squares = numbers.map(function(num) {
```

```
    return num * num;
});
console.log(squares); // Outputs: [1, 4, 9, 16]
```

- The `map()` method transforms each element of the `numbers` array by squaring it, and returns a new array `squares`.

---

9. filter()

- **Purpose:** Creates a new array with all elements that pass the test implemented by the provided function.
- **Syntax:** `array.filter(callback)`

Example:
```
let numbers = [1, 2, 3, 4, 5];
let evenNumbers = numbers.filter(function(num) {
    return num % 2 === 0;
});
console.log(evenNumbers); // Outputs: [2, 4]
```

- The `filter()` method filters the `numbers` array to include only even numbers, and returns a new array `evenNumbers`.

---

10. reduce()

- **Purpose:** Applies a function against an accumulator and each element in the array (from left to right) to reduce it to a single value.
- **Syntax:** `array.reduce(callback, initialValue)`

Example:
```
let numbers = [1, 2, 3, 4];
let sum = numbers.reduce(function(accumulator, num) {
    return accumulator + num;
}, 0);
console.log(sum); // Outputs: 10
```

- The `reduce()` method calculates the sum of the elements in the `numbers` array. It starts with an accumulator of 0 and adds each number in the array.

Summary of Common Array Methods:

Method	Purpose
push()	Adds one or more elements to the end of an array.
pop()	Removes the last element from an array and returns it.
shift()	Removes the first element from an array and returns it.
unshift()	Adds one or more elements to the beginning of an array.
slice()	Returns a shallow copy of a portion of an array.
splice()	Changes the contents of an array by removing, replacing, or adding elements.
forEach()	Executes a function once for each element in the array.
map()	Creates a new array populated with the results of calling a provided function on each element.
filter()	Creates a new array with all elements that pass the test in the provided function.
reduce()	Reduces the array to a single value by applying a function against an accumulator and each element.

These methods are essential tools for manipulating arrays and working with data effectively in JavaScript. They allow you to easily add, remove, modify, and iterate over array elements to meet your needs.

Understanding Objects and Properties

Objects are essential structures in JavaScript that allow you to store collections of data and more complex entities. They are versatile and can hold properties (values associated with keys) and methods (functions associated with an object). Below is a detailed explanation of objects and their operations.

Creating Objects

Objects in JavaScript are created using **curly braces** {}. Inside the curly braces, properties and methods are defined as key-value pairs.

- **Properties** are values associated with a key.
- **Methods** are functions that belong to the object.

Example of an Object:
```
let person = {
    name: "John",
    age: 30,
    greet: function() {
        console.log("Hello, " + this.name);
    }
};
```

- **Properties:**
  - name: Stores the name of the person.
  - age: Stores the age of the person.
- **Method:**
  - greet: A method that logs a greeting message using the name property.

Accessing Object Properties

There are two main ways to access properties of an object: **dot notation** and **bracket notation**.

1. Dot Notation

Dot notation is the most common and straightforward method to access object properties.

```
console.log(person.name); // Outputs: John
```
2. Bracket Notation

Bracket notation is useful when property names are dynamic or contain spaces.

```
console.log(person["age"]); // Outputs: 30
```

Bracket notation is also helpful when the property name is not a valid identifier (such as a property name with spaces or special characters).

Modifying Object Properties

You can **modify** existing properties or **add** new properties to an object using both dot and bracket notation.

Example: Modifying and Adding Properties
```
// Modifying an existing property
person.age = 31;
```

```
// Adding a new property
person.city = "New York";

console.log(person);
// Outputs: { name: "John", age: 31, greet: [Function], city: "New York" }
```

In this example:

- The `age` property is modified to `31`.
- The `city` property is added to the object with the value `"New York"`.

Object Methods

An **object method** is a function that is defined as part of an object. The `this` keyword inside a method refers to the object the method belongs to.

Example: Object with Method
```
let car = {
    make: "Toyota",
    model: "Corolla",
    year: 2020,
    displayInfo: function() {
        console.log(this.make + " " + this.model + " (" + this.year + ")");
    }
};

car.displayInfo(); // Outputs: Toyota Corolla (2020)
```

Here, `displayInfo` is a method of the `car` object. The `this` keyword refers to the `car` object itself.

Deleting Object Properties

You can **delete** a property from an object using the `delete` operator. This operation removes the property from the object.

Example: Deleting a Property
```
delete person.city;
console.log(person);
// Outputs: { name: "John", age: 31, greet: [Function] }
```

In this example, the `city` property is deleted from the `person` object.

Iterating Through Object Properties

To iterate through an object's properties, you can use a `for...in` loop. This loop will go through each key in the object, and you can access both the key and its value.

Example: Iterating Through Object Properties
```
let person = {
    name: "John",
    age: 30,
    country: "USA"
};

for (let key in person) {
    console.log(key + ": " + person[key]);
}
// Outputs:
// name: John
// age: 30
// country: USA
```

In the above example:

- The `for...in` loop iterates through the `person` object.
- `key` represents the property name, and `person[key]` accesses the value of the property.

Object Destructuring

Object destructuring allows you to extract values from an object and assign them to variables in a concise way. This is especially helpful when you want to access specific properties without referencing the object multiple times.

Example: Object Destructuring
```
let person = {
    name: "John",
    age: 30,
    city: "New York"
};

let { name, age } = person;
console.log(name); // Outputs: John
console.log(age);  // Outputs: 30
```

In this example:

- The properties `name` and `age` are **extracted** from the `person` object and assigned to new variables `name` and `age`.
- This eliminates the need to write `person.name` and `person.age` repeatedly.

Summary

- **Arrays** in JavaScript are used to store multiple values in a single variable. They are indexed by numbers and can be manipulated using a variety of array methods like `push()`, `pop()`, `shift()`, `unshift()`, and more.
- **Objects** are collections of key-value pairs, where the keys are usually strings (or symbols) and the values can be any data type, including other objects or functions. Objects are useful for representing more complex data structures.

By understanding arrays and objects, you can organize and manipulate your data efficiently in JavaScript.

25 multiple-choice questions (MCQs) on the topics: **Introduction to Arrays**, **Array Methods and Operations**, and **Understanding Objects and Properties**.

Introduction to Arrays

1. **Which of the following is the correct way to define an array in JavaScript?**
   - a) `let arr = array(1, 2, 3);`
   - b) `let arr = [1, 2, 3];`
   - c) `let arr = (1, 2, 3);`
   - d) `let arr = new Array(1, 2, 3);`

   Answer: b) `let arr = [1, 2, 3];`

2. **What does `arr.length` represent in JavaScript?**
   - a) The first element of the array
   - b) The number of elements in the array
   - c) The last element of the array
   - d) The index of the first element

   Answer: b) The number of elements in the array

3. **Which method is used to access the first element of an array?**
   - a) `arr.get(0)`
   - b) `arr[0]`
   - c) `arr.first()`
   - d) `arr.getFirst()`

   Answer: b) `arr[0]`

4. **What is the index of the last element in the array `let arr = [1, 2, 3, 4]`?**
   - a) 4
   - b) 3
   - c) 2
   - d) 0

Answer: b) 3

5. **Which of the following is NOT a valid way to create an array in JavaScript?**
    - a) `let arr = []`
    - b) `let arr = new Array()`
    - c) `let arr = Array.new()`
    - d) `let arr = Array(3)`

Answer: c) `let arr = Array.new()`

Array Methods and Operations

6. **What does the `push()` method do in an array?**
    - a) Adds an element at the beginning of the array
    - b) Removes the first element from the array
    - c) Adds an element to the end of the array
    - d) Removes the last element from the array

Answer: c) Adds an element to the end of the array

7. **What will be the output of the following code?**

```
let arr = [1, 2, 3];
arr.pop();
console.log(arr);
```

    - a) `[1, 2]`
    - b) `[2, 3]`
    - c) `[1, 2, 3]`
    - d) `[3]`

Answer: a) `[1, 2]`

8. **Which method is used to remove the first element from an array?**
    - a) `pop()`
    - b) `shift()`
    - c) `slice()`
    - d) `unshift()`

Answer: b) `shift()`

9. **What will the following code return?**

```
let arr = [1, 2, 3];
arr.unshift(0);
console.log(arr);
```

o a) `[1, 2, 3, 0]`
o b) `[0, 1, 2, 3]`
o c) `[1, 2, 3]`
o d) `[0]`

Answer: b) `[0, 1, 2, 3]`

10. **Which method creates a new array by slicing an existing one?**
    o a) `splice()`
    o b) `slice()`
    o c) `map()`
    o d) `forEach()`

Answer: b) `slice()`

11. **What does the `map()` method do in JavaScript?**
    o a) Iterates through the array and changes elements in place
    o b) Creates a new array populated with the results of applying a function to every element
    o c) Reverses the elements of an array
    o d) Removes the first element from an array

Answer: b) Creates a new array populated with the results of applying a function to every element

12. **What will the following code output?**

```
let arr = [1, 2, 3, 4];
let result = arr.filter(num => num % 2 === 0);
console.log(result);
```

    o a) `[1, 3]`
    o b) `[2, 4]`
    o c) `[1, 2, 3]`
    o d) `[4]`

Answer: b) `[2, 4]`

13. **Which method is used to reduce an array to a single value in JavaScript?**
    o a) `reduce()`
    o b) `map()`
    o c) `join()`
    o d) `split()`

Answer: a) `reduce()`

14. **What does the `splice()` method do in an array?**
    - o a) Removes elements from the end of an array
    - o b) Creates a shallow copy of an array
    - o c) Adds or removes elements from a specific index
    - o d) Combines two arrays into one

    Answer: c) Adds or removes elements from a specific index

15. **Which of the following methods is used to loop over the elements of an array without modifying the array?**
    - o a) `forEach()`
    - o b) `map()`
    - o c) `splice()`
    - o d) `slice()`

    Answer: a) `forEach()`

Understanding Objects and Properties

16. **How do you access the value of a property in an object using dot notation?**
    - o a) `object.property`
    - o b) `object["property"]`
    - o c) `object[property]`
    - o d) `object{property}`

    Answer: a) `object.property`

17. **Which of the following is a valid way to define an object in JavaScript?**
    - o a) `let person = { name: "John", age: 30 };`
    - o b) `let person = (name: "John", age: 30);`
    - o c) `let person = name: "John", age: 30;`
    - o d) `let person = [name: "John", age: 30];`

    Answer: a) `let person = { name: "John", age: 30 };`

18. **What does the `delete` operator do in relation to objects?**
    - o a) Removes a method from an object
    - o b) Removes a property from an object
    - o c) Deletes the entire object
    - o d) Removes an element from an array

    Answer: b) Removes a property from an object

19. **What will be the output of the following code?**

    ```
    let person = { name: "Alice", age: 25 };
    ```

```
delete person.age;
console.log(person);
```

- o a) { name: "Alice" }
- o b) { age: 25 }
- o c) { name: "Alice", age: 25 }
- o d) undefined

Answer: a) { name: "Alice" }

20. **What will the following code output?**

```
let person = { name: "John", age: 30 };
console.log(person["name"]);
```

- o a) undefined
- o b) name
- o c) John
- o d) 30

Answer: c) John

21. **Which of the following is correct to access an object's property using bracket notation?**
    - o a) object.property
    - o b) object["property"]
    - o c) object(property)
    - o d) object.get("property")

Answer: b) object["property"]

22. **How do you add a new property to an object in JavaScript?**
    - o a) object.addProperty("key", value);
    - o b) object["key"] = value;
    - o c) object.add("key", value);
    - o d) object.push("key", value);

Answer: b) object["key"] = value;

23. **Which of the following is used to iterate over an object's properties?**
    - o a) forEach()
    - o b) for...in
    - o c) map()
    - o d) for...of

Answer: b) for...in

24. **What will the following code return?**

```
let car = { make: "Toyota", model: "Corolla", year: 2020 };
let { make, model } = car;
console.log(make, model);
```

- o **a)** `Toyota, Corolla`
- o **b)** `{ make, model }`
- o **c)** `undefined, undefined`
- o **d)** `Toyota`

Answer: a) `Toyota, Corolla`

25. **What is the `this` keyword inside a method of an object referring to?**
- o a) The method itself
- o b) The object that the method belongs to
- o c) The global object
- o d) Undefined

Answer: b) The object that the method belongs to

CHAPTER-5

ADVANCED JAVASCRIPT CONCEPTS

1. Closures and Callback Functions

What are Closures?

A **closure** is a function that "remembers" its lexical scope (the environment in which it was defined), even after the outer function has finished executing. In simpler terms, closures allow an inner function to access variables and parameters from its outer function even after the outer function has returned.

This is possible because JavaScript functions create closures when they are defined. The inner function retains access to the outer function's variables, even after the outer function has completed execution. This characteristic is what makes closures powerful.

How Closures Work:

For a closure to occur, two main conditions must be met:

1. **An inner function is defined** inside an outer function.
2. The inner function **retains access to the outer function's variables**, even after the outer function has completed execution.

This is possible because of the **lexical scoping** of JavaScript, which refers to the fact that functions have access to the variables and parameters defined in the scope in which they were created.

Example of Closures:
```
function outerFunction() {
    let count = 0;   // This is a variable inside the outer function

    function innerFunction() {
        count++;   // Accesses the 'count' variable from the outer function
        console.log(count);   // Prints the current value of 'count'
    }

    return innerFunction;   // Returns the inner function, forming a closure
}

const increment = outerFunction();   // outerFunction returns innerFunction
increment();   // Outputs: 1
increment();   // Outputs: 2
increment();   // Outputs: 3
```

Explanation:

- **outerFunction** defines a variable `count` and an inner function `innerFunction()`.

- **innerFunction** has access to the variable count, which was defined in the **outer scope**.
- When outerFunction() is called, it returns innerFunction(), which "remembers" the count variable from the outer scope.
- Even though the outer function has already finished executing, innerFunction still has access to count and can modify it each time it's called.
- **Every time increment() is called**, it increases the value of count, demonstrating how the closure "remembers" the state of the outer function's variables.

Key Takeaways:

- Closures are powerful because they allow functions to have private data (like the count variable in the example) that can be manipulated even after the outer function has completed execution.
- Closures are commonly used in JavaScript to create private variables or to implement functions that need to maintain state across multiple invocations.

2. Callback Functions in JavaScript

What are Callback Functions?

A **callback function** is a function passed as an argument to another function and is typically executed **later** in the program. Callbacks are often used for handling asynchronous operations, such as reading files, fetching data from APIs, or responding to events (like button clicks).

In JavaScript, many functions work asynchronously (e.g., **setTimeout, event listeners, fetch requests**, etc.), and callbacks allow you to define what should happen once these operations are complete.

Example of a Callback Function:
```
function greet(name, callback) {
    console.log('Hello, ' + name);  // Prints the greeting message
    callback();  // Executes the callback function after the greeting
}

function afterGreet() {
    console.log('Welcome to the world of JavaScript!');
}

greet('Alice', afterGreet);
// Outputs:
// Hello, Alice
// Welcome to the world of JavaScript!
```

Explanation:

- The greet() function accepts two arguments: a name and a callback function.
- It first logs a greeting message (Hello, Alice), and then calls the callback() function (which is afterGreet()).

- **afterGreet()** is the callback function, and it is executed after the greeting is logged.
- The **callback function** is executed at a later time, allowing us to chain functions together and manage the order of execution.

Callback Functions in Asynchronous Operations:

One of the most common uses of callback functions is in **asynchronous operations**, where you don't know exactly when the operation will complete (e.g., fetching data from an API). Here's an example with **setTimeout()** (which simulates a delayed operation):

```
function simulateAsyncOperation(callback) {
    console.log("Starting operation...");

    // Simulate a 2-second delay (asynchronous task)
    setTimeout(function() {
        console.log("Operation complete.");
        callback();  // Calls the callback function after 2 seconds
    }, 2000);
}

function onComplete() {
    console.log("This is the callback function running after the async
operation.");
}

simulateAsyncOperation(onComplete);
// Outputs:
// Starting operation...
// Operation complete.
// This is the callback function running after the async operation.
```

Explanation:

- **simulateAsyncOperation()** simulates a delayed operation (e.g., fetching data), using setTimeout to create a 2-second delay.
- After the delay, the callback function (onComplete()) is executed.
- **Callbacks** allow us to define what should happen once the asynchronous operation (in this case, the 2-second timeout) has finished.

Key Takeaways:

- Callback functions allow you to **defer execution** of a function until a certain condition is met or an asynchronous operation completes.
- Callbacks are essential in JavaScript for managing tasks like handling events or processing asynchronous data, and they help ensure that your code doesn't block or freeze while waiting for an operation to finish.

2. Promises and Asynchronous JavaScript

In JavaScript, promises are used to handle asynchronous operations, such as fetching data from a server, reading files, or performing other non-blocking tasks. Promises help manage these operations more effectively by allowing you to handle success or failure once the operation is complete.

1. What Are Promises?

A **promise** is an object that represents the eventual completion (or failure) of an asynchronous operation. Think of it as a placeholder for a result that will eventually be returned after some time (or upon failure).

Promises have three possible states:

1. **Pending**: The promise is still in progress, i.e., the asynchronous operation has not yet completed.
2. **Fulfilled**: The operation was successful, and the promise is now resolved.
3. **Rejected**: The operation failed, and the promise is rejected.

2. Creating a Promise

You can create a promise in JavaScript using the `Promise` constructor, which accepts a **callback function** with two parameters: `resolve` and `reject`.

- `resolve(value)`: This function is called when the asynchronous operation is successful.
- `reject(error)`: This function is called if the operation fails.

Here's an example:

Example: Creating a Simple Promise
```javascript
let myPromise = new Promise(function(resolve, reject) {
    let success = true;  // Simulate success or failure

    if(success) {
        resolve("The operation was successful!");  // Resolving the promise
    } else {
        reject("The operation failed.");  // Rejecting the promise
    }
});

myPromise
    .then(function(result) {
        console.log(result);  // Executes if the promise is resolved
```

```
})
.catch(function(error) {
    console.log(error);    // Executes if the promise is rejected
});
```

Explanation:

1. **Creating the Promise**:
   - The `new Promise()` constructor creates a promise. Inside, we define the asynchronous logic (in this case, a simple `success` variable).
2. **Resolve or Reject**:
   - If the `success` variable is true, the promise is resolved with a success message using `resolve()`.
   - If `success` is false, the promise is rejected with an error message using `reject()`.
3. **Handling the Promise**:
   - The `.then()` method is used to handle the success case when the promise is resolved.
   - The `.catch()` method is used to handle the failure case when the promise is rejected.

3. Using Promises with Asynchronous Code

Promises are extremely useful for handling asynchronous operations like fetching data from a server. They help avoid callback hell (nested callbacks) and provide a cleaner, more manageable way of dealing with asynchronous logic.

Example: Using Promises for Asynchronous Operations (e.g., Fetching Data)

```
function fetchData(url) {
    return new Promise(function(resolve, reject) {
        setTimeout(() => {
            let success = true;    // Simulate success or failure
            if(success) {
                resolve("Data fetched successfully from " + url);    // Resolve
the promise with data
            } else {
                reject("Failed to fetch data from " + url);    // Reject the
promise with an error
            }
        }, 2000);    // Simulate a delay of 2 seconds
    });
}

fetchData("https://api.example.com")
    .then(function(data) {
        console.log(data);    // Executes if the promise is resolved
    })
    .catch(function(error) {
        console.log(error);    // Executes if the promise is rejected
    });
```

Explanation:

1. **Creating the `fetchData` Promise:**
   - The `fetchData` function simulates an API call using `setTimeout()` to introduce a 2-second delay.
   - Inside the promise, we simulate the result with a success/failure variable (`success`).
   - If the `success` variable is true, the promise is resolved with a message indicating that data was fetched successfully.
   - If `success` is false, the promise is rejected, simulating an error while fetching data.
2. **Using `.then()` and `.catch()`:**
   - `.then()` is used to handle the resolved promise and process the data returned.
   - `.catch()` is used to handle any errors if the promise is rejected.

---

4. Promise Chaining

Promises allow you to chain multiple `.then()` calls, making it easier to work with asynchronous code sequentially. This is useful when you need to perform a series of asynchronous operations in a specific order.

Example: Promise Chaining
```
function fetchData(url) {
    return new Promise(function(resolve, reject) {
        setTimeout(() => {
            let success = true;
            if(success) {
                resolve("Data fetched successfully from " + url);
            } else {
                reject("Failed to fetch data from " + url);
            }
        }, 2000);
    });
}

fetchData("https://api.example.com")
    .then(function(data) {
        console.log(data);   // First then() handles the resolved promise
        return fetchData("https://api.example.com/next");   // Chaining
another async task
    })
    .then(function(nextData) {
        console.log(nextData);   // Second then() handles the next resolved
promise
    })
    .catch(function(error) {
        console.log(error);   // Handles any errors from either promise
    });
```
Explanation:

- The first `.then()` handles the first resolved promise (fetching the data from the first URL).

- The second `.then()` handles the next resolved promise (fetching data from a second URL), which is chained after the first.
- If there's any error in any promise (like failure to fetch data), the `.catch()` method will handle it.

---

5. Promise.all() and Promise.race()

JavaScript also provides some utilities for handling multiple promises at once.

- **`Promise.all()`**: This method takes an array of promises and returns a single promise that resolves when all the input promises have been resolved, or rejects when any of the input promises is rejected.
- **`Promise.race()`**: This method takes an array of promises and returns a promise that resolves or rejects as soon as any of the input promises resolves or rejects.

Example: Using `Promise.all()`
```
function fetchData(url) {
    return new Promise(function(resolve, reject) {
        setTimeout(() => {
            resolve("Data fetched from " + url);
        }, Math.random() * 2000);  // Random delay
    });
}

Promise.all([
    fetchData("https://api.example.com"),
    fetchData("https://api.example2.com")
])
.then(function(results) {
    console.log(results);  // ["Data fetched from https://api.example.com",
"Data fetched from https://api.example2.com"]
})
.catch(function(error) {
    console.log(error);
});
```

Explanation:

- `Promise.all()` waits for all the promises to resolve and returns an array of results once all promises have successfully resolved.

---

3. Error Handling (try, catch)

Error handling in JavaScript is crucial for writing robust code that can gracefully handle unexpected situations, like invalid input, failed network requests, or other runtime issues. JavaScript provides the `try...catch` statement, which allows you to handle errors effectively.

---

1. The `try...catch` Block

The `try...catch` block is a fundamental mechanism in JavaScript to handle errors. It allows you to attempt a block of code and catch any errors that occur during execution. Here's how it works:

- **`try` block**: Contains the code that might throw an error.
- **`catch` block**: Contains the code that handles the error if it occurs during the execution of the `try` block.
- **`finally` block** (optional): Contains code that runs regardless of whether an error occurred or not. This is useful for clean-up tasks like closing files, releasing resources, etc.

Syntax of `try...catch`:

```
try {
    // Code that may throw an error
} catch (error) {
    // Code that handles the error
} finally {
    // Code that will run regardless of an error (optional)
}
```

Basic Example of `try...catch`:

```
try {
    let result = someFunction();   // This may throw an error if someFunction
is not defined
    console.log(result);
} catch (error) {
    console.error("An error occurred: " + error.message);   // Handles the
error
}
```
Explanation:

- If `someFunction()` is not defined or throws an error, the `catch` block will be triggered.
- The `catch` block catches the error and the error object contains information about the error. The `error.message` property is logged to the console, displaying the error message.

---

2. Using `try...catch` with Asynchronous Code (async/await)

Handling errors in asynchronous code (e.g., fetching data, reading files) is also very important. Since `async` functions return a **promise**, you can use `try...catch` blocks in combination with `async/await` to handle errors effectively in asynchronous code.

Example: Using `try...catch` with Async/Await:

```
async function fetchData() {
    try {
        let response = await fetch("https://api.example.com/data");
        let data = await response.json();
        console.log(data);  // Handle the fetched data
    } catch (error) {
        console.error("Error fetching data:", error);  // Handle the error if
the fetch fails
    }
}

fetchData();
```

Explanation:

- The `fetchData()` function is an `async` function that uses `await` to wait for the `fetch()` request to complete.
- If an error occurs during the fetch operation (e.g., a network issue or invalid URL), the `catch` block will catch the error, and the error will be logged to the console.

In this case, the error could be an exception raised by `fetch()` or `response.json()` if there is an issue with the data format.

3. Throwing Custom Errors

You can also create your own custom errors using the `throw` keyword inside the `try` block. This is especially useful for scenarios where you want to handle specific business logic errors or invalid input.

Example: Throwing Custom Errors:

```
function divideNumbers(a, b) {
    try {
        if (b === 0) {
            throw new Error("Cannot divide by zero!");  // Throwing a custom
error
        }
        console.log(a / b);
    } catch (error) {
        console.error(error.message);  // Catching and logging the error
message
    }
}
```

```
divideNumbers(10, 0);   // Outputs: Cannot divide by zero!
```
Explanation:

- In the `divideNumbers()` function, we check if `b` is zero before performing the division.
- If `b` is zero, we manually throw an error using `throw new Error("Cannot divide by zero!")`.
- The `catch` block catches the error, and the error message is logged to the console.

You can create more specific errors by using custom messages or even creating custom error classes.

4. Using the `finally` Block

The `finally` block is an optional part of the `try...catch` structure that runs regardless of whether an error was thrown or not. This makes it useful for cleanup operations such as closing files, releasing resources, or stopping animations.

Example: Using `finally`:
```
function readFile() {
    try {
        let fileData = readFileSync('data.txt');   // Simulated file reading
operation
        console.log(fileData);
    } catch (error) {
        console.error("An error occurred while reading the file: " +
error.message);
    } finally {
        console.log("Cleanup tasks (e.g., closing file) are performed
here.");
    }
}

readFile();
```
Explanation:

- The `finally` block runs regardless of whether the file reading operation succeeds or fails.
- This is useful for cleanup operations, such as closing file streams, even if an error occurs.

5. The `error` Object

The `error` object in the `catch` block contains useful information about the error. This object has several properties:

- **message**: The error message string (e.g., `"Cannot divide by zero!"`).

- **name**: The name of the error (e.g., `"TypeError"`, `"ReferenceError"`).
- **stack**: The stack trace, which provides details on where the error occurred in the code.

Example: Accessing `error` Object Properties:
```
try {
    let result = someNonExistentFunction();
} catch (error) {
    console.error("Error message: " + error.message);
    console.error("Error stack: " + error.stack);
}
```
Explanation:

- `error.message` will provide the error message (e.g., "someNonExistentFunction is not defined").
- `error.stack` provides the stack trace, which can help you debug where the error occurred in the code.

6. Best Practices for Error Handling

- **Handle errors gracefully**: Always anticipate potential errors and handle them appropriately, rather than letting them crash the application.
- **Be specific in your error messages**: Provide meaningful messages that help developers or users understand what went wrong.
- **Avoid silent failures**: Don't catch errors without handling them or logging them. Silent failures can make it difficult to debug issues.
- **Use `finally` for cleanup**: Use the `finally` block for cleanup operations that should run whether an error occurs or not.
- **Create custom errors**: Throw custom errors for business logic or validation errors, rather than relying on generic ones.

Summary of Key Concepts:

1. **Closures** allow functions to remember and access variables from their outer scope even after the outer function has finished execution.
2. **Callback Functions** are functions passed as arguments to other functions, executed once the original function completes.
3. **Promises** represent the result of an asynchronous operation, allowing you to handle success (`.then()`) or failure (`.catch()`).
4. **Error Handling (try, catch)** is essential for catching and managing errors during code execution, especially in asynchronous code.

These concepts form the foundation of handling asynchronous operations, managing scope, and handling errors in JavaScript, making your code more robust and maintainable.

25 multiple-choice questions (MCQs) based on the topics **Closures and Callback Functions, Promises and Asynchronous JavaScript**, and **Error Handling (try, catch)**:

Closures and Callback Functions

1. **What is a closure in JavaScript?**
   - ○ A) A function that is declared inside another function and can access its outer function's variables.
   - ○ B) A method to call another function asynchronously.
   - ○ C) A function that doesn't return any value.
   - ○ D) A function that is used for error handling.

   Answer: A

2. **Which of the following is an example of a closure in JavaScript?**
   - ○ A) `let x = 10; function foo() { console.log(x); }`
   - ○ B) `function outer() { let count = 0; return function inner() { count++; console.log(count); }; }`
   - ○ C) `let a = (x, y) => x + y;`
   - ○ D) `function bar() { return 5; }`

   Answer: B

3. **Which of the following is NOT a characteristic of closures?**
   - ○ A) They have access to variables from the outer function.
   - ○ B) They can return a function.
   - ○ C) They only execute once.
   - ○ D) They remember the environment in which they were created.

   Answer: C

4. **What does the following JavaScript code log to the console?**

   ```
   function outer() {
       let count = 0;
       return function inner() {
           count++;
           console.log(count);
       };
   }
   const increment = outer();
   increment();
   increment();
   ```

   - ○ A) 1 1
   - ○ B) 1 2

- C) 0 1
- D) 0 0

Answer: B

5. **What is a callback function in JavaScript?**
   - A) A function that is called when another function is executed synchronously.
   - B) A function that is passed as an argument to another function and executed later.
   - C) A function that handles errors.
   - D) A function that stops the program.

Answer: B

6. **Which of the following is a common use of callback functions?**
   - A) Error handling
   - B) Delayed execution, such as with `setTimeout()`
   - C) Returning values from functions
   - D) Creating loops

Answer: B

7. **Which of the following callbacks will execute after 2 seconds?**

```
setTimeout(function() {
    console.log("Hello!");
}, 2000);
```

   - A) Immediately
   - B) After 5 seconds
   - C) After 2 seconds
   - D) Never

Answer: C

8. **In the following example, what will be logged first?**

```
function greet(name, callback) {
    console.log('Hello, ' + name);
    callback();
}

function afterGreet() {
    console.log('Welcome!');
}

greet('Alice', afterGreet);
```

- o **A)** `Welcome!`
- o **B)** `Hello, Alice`
- o **C)** `Hello, Alice Welcome!`
- o **D)** `afterGreet`

Answer: B

9. **What happens if a callback function is passed to an asynchronous function but does not execute?**
   - o A) It will execute immediately.
   - o B) It will be logged as an error.
   - o C) It will be ignored, and no result will be produced.
   - o D) It will be executed after a delay.

Answer: C

10. **Which of the following is the primary purpose of a callback function?**

- A) To add functionality to a function.
- B) To return a value from a function.
- C) To execute a function after a certain event or task completes.
- D) To stop the execution of a function.

Answer: C

Promises and Asynchronous JavaScript

11. **What is the state of a promise when the operation is still in progress?**

- A) Pending
- B) Fulfilled
- C) Rejected
- D) None of the above

Answer: A

12. **Which method is used to handle the resolved value of a promise?**

- A) `catch()`
- B) `then()`
- C) `resolve()`
- D) `reject()`

Answer: B

13. Which method is used to handle a promise that has been rejected?

- A) `catch()`
- B) `then()`
- C) `resolve()`
- D) `finally()`

Answer: A

14. What does the following code output?

```
let promise = new Promise((resolve, reject) => {
    let success = true;
    if (success) {
        resolve("Success!");
    } else {
        reject("Failure!");
    }
});

promise
    .then(result => console.log(result))
    .catch(error => console.log(error));
```

- A) `Success!`
- B) `Failure!`
- C) `undefined`
- D) An error is thrown.

Answer: A

15. Which of the following statements about promises is true?

- A) A promise can only be in one of two states: resolved or rejected.
- B) A promise can only be in one state at a time: pending.
- C) A promise can change its state back and forth between resolved and rejected.
- D) Promises are synchronous in nature.

Answer: A

16. What will be logged to the console after 2 seconds when using this code?

```
let myPromise = new Promise((resolve, reject) => {
    setTimeout(() => resolve("Data received"), 2000);
});

myPromise.then(result => console.log(result));
```

- A) `Data received`

- B) `undefined`
- C) `Timeout exceeded`
- D) `Promise error`

Answer: A

17. **What is the purpose of the `finally()` method in promises?**

- A) It executes code only if the promise is fulfilled.
- B) It executes code only if the promise is rejected.
- C) It executes code regardless of whether the promise is fulfilled or rejected.
- D) It pauses the promise execution.

Answer: C

18. **Which function allows you to handle multiple promises simultaneously and wait for all of them to resolve?**

- A) `Promise.all()`
- B) `Promise.then()`
- C) `Promise.catch()`
- D) `Promise.any()`

Answer: A

19. **In the following code, what will be logged?**

```
let promise1 = Promise.resolve(1);
let promise2 = Promise.resolve(2);

Promise.all([promise1, promise2])
    .then(result => console.log(result));
```

- A) `[1, 2]`
- B) `1`
- C) `2`
- D) `undefined`

Answer: A

20. **How does the `await` keyword work in asynchronous JavaScript?**

- A) It pauses the function execution until a promise is resolved.
- B) It executes promises synchronously.
- C) It handles errors in promises.
- D) It waits for a callback to complete.

Answer: A

Error Handling (try, catch)

21. **What happens when an error occurs in the `try` block in JavaScript?**

- A) The program stops immediately.
- B) The `catch` block is executed.
- C) The `finally` block is skipped.
- D) The program ignores the error.

Answer: B

22. **Which block in the `try...catch` statement runs regardless of an error occurring?**

- A) `catch`
- B) `finally`
- C) `try`
- D) None of the above

Answer: B

23. **What is the purpose of the `throw` keyword in JavaScript?**

- A) To return a value from a function.
- B) To stop the program execution.
- C) To manually throw an error.
- D) To handle caught errors.

Answer: C

24. Which of the following statements about `try...catch` is correct?

- A) Errors in the `catch` block can't be caught by another `catch` block.
- B) `finally` is optional but can be used for cleanup operations.
- C) `catch` is used to define the code to be executed after a promise is resolved.
- D) The `catch` block is executed only if there is no error in the `try` block.

Answer: B

25. What will this code output?

```
try {
    throw new Error("Custom error");
} catch (error) {
    console.log(error.message);
}
```

- A) `undefined`
- B) `Custom error`
- C) `Error: Custom error`
- D) `Custom error: error`

Answer: B

CHAPTER-6

Understanding the DOM (Document Object Model)

The **Document Object Model (DOM)** is a critical concept in web development. It provides a structured representation of the document and a way to interact with the content through programming languages, most commonly **JavaScript**. Essentially, it allows developers to manipulate the document's structure, content, and styling dynamically. Understanding the DOM is essential for building interactive and dynamic web applications.

What Is the DOM?

The **DOM** represents the structure of an HTML or XML document as a tree of objects, where each object corresponds to a part of the document. The DOM allows JavaScript to read and manipulate elements, their attributes, text content, and more. It is often referred to as an **API** (Application Programming Interface) that enables scripts to interact with the content and structure of a webpage.

The **DOM Tree** is a hierarchical structure in which:

- The **document** is the root.
- Each HTML element (e.g., <html>, <body>, <p>, etc.) is a node within the tree.
- Every HTML tag is treated as an **object** in the DOM, and these objects can be accessed, changed, or deleted through JavaScript.

Key Concepts of the DOM

1. **Document (Root Object)**:
   - The document object is the root of the DOM tree. It represents the entire webpage.
   - It's the starting point for accessing all other parts of the document. From here, you can access elements, attributes, and text nodes within the page.
2. **Elements (Nodes)**:
   - HTML tags such as <div>, <p>, <a>, <h1>, etc., are treated as **elements** in the DOM. These elements are **nodes** in the DOM tree.
   - Each element node can have child nodes, attributes, and text content.
   - Elements are objects in JavaScript and can be manipulated using various DOM methods like getElementById, getElementsByClassName, etc.
3. **Attributes**:
   - Attributes are properties associated with HTML elements, such as id, class, href, src, alt, etc.
   - These attributes define the behavior or style of the element. For instance, the id attribute uniquely identifies an element, and href defines the destination URL for an anchor <a> tag.

o   JavaScript allows you to access, modify, and delete attributes of an element using methods like `getAttribute`, `setAttribute`, and `removeAttribute`.

4. **Text Nodes**:
   o   A **text node** contains the text content of an element.
   o   In the DOM, text is treated as a separate type of node. For example, in `<p>Hello, World!</p>`, the text `"Hello, World!"` is a **text node**.
   o   JavaScript provides ways to modify the text content of an element via properties like `textContent` and `innerHTML`.

DOM Tree Structure

The **DOM Tree** is a hierarchical model of the document's structure. The tree starts with the `document` object, and each HTML element becomes a child of its parent element in the hierarchy.

Here is an example of how the DOM represents an HTML document structure:

Example HTML:
```
<!DOCTYPE html>
<html>
<head>
    <title>My Web Page</title>
</head>
<body>
    <h1>Welcome to my website</h1>
    <p id="intro">This is an introduction paragraph.</p>
    <button id="changeText">Change Text</button>
</body>
</html>
```
DOM Tree Representation:
```
document
    └── html
          ├── head
          │     └── title
          │           └── "My Web Page"
          └── body
                ├── h1
                │     └── "Welcome to my website"
                ├── p (id="intro")
                │     └── "This is an introduction paragraph."
                └── button (id="changeText")
                      └── "Change Text"
```

*   **Root Element**: The `document` is the root object.
*   **Element Nodes**: `<html>`, `<head>`, `<title>`, `<body>`, `<h1>`, `<p>`, and `<button>` are all nodes in the DOM tree.
*   **Text Nodes**: `"My Web Page"`, `"Welcome to my website"`, `"This is an introduction paragraph"`, and `"Change Text"` are text nodes.
*   **Attributes**: The `<p>` element has an `id` attribute with the value `"intro"`, and the `<button>` element has an `id` attribute with the value `"changeText"`.

Accessing the DOM in JavaScript

To interact with the DOM in JavaScript, you use the `document` object and various DOM methods that allow you to select and manipulate elements.

Selecting Elements

JavaScript provides several methods to access DOM elements:

1. **`getElementById(id)`**: Selects an element by its `id` attribute. This method returns the first matching element.

   ```
   let intro = document.getElementById("intro");
   console.log(intro); // <p id="intro">This is an introduction
   paragraph.</p>
   ```

2. **`getElementsByClassName(className)`**: Selects all elements with the specified class. It returns an HTMLCollection.

   ```
   let paragraphs = document.getElementsByClassName("intro-text");
   console.log(paragraphs); // HTMLCollection of elements with class
   "intro-text"
   ```

3. **`getElementsByTagName(tagName)`**: Selects all elements with a specified tag name. It returns an HTMLCollection.

   ```
   let paragraphs = document.getElementsByTagName("p");
   console.log(paragraphs); // HTMLCollection of all <p> elements
   ```

4. **`querySelector(selector)`**: Selects the first element matching the CSS selector. This method allows for more complex queries.

   ```
   let firstParagraph = document.querySelector("p");
   console.log(firstParagraph); // <p id="intro">This is an introduction
   paragraph.</p>
   ```

5. **`querySelectorAll(selector)`**: Selects all elements matching the CSS selector. It returns a NodeList.

   ```
   let allParagraphs = document.querySelectorAll("p");
   console.log(allParagraphs); // NodeList of all <p> elements
   ```

Manipulating Elements

Once you've selected an element, you can modify its content, attributes, or styles.

1. **Change the text content of an element:**

```
let intro = document.getElementById("intro");
intro.textContent = "This is the updated text.";
```

2. **Change the HTML content of an element**:

```
let intro = document.getElementById("intro");
intro.innerHTML = "<b>This is a bold introduction.</b>";
```

3. **Change an element's style**:

```
let heading = document.querySelector("h1");
heading.style.color = "blue"; // Change the text color to blue
```

4. **Change an element's attribute**:

```
let button = document.getElementById("changeText");
button.setAttribute("disabled", "true"); // Disable the button
```

5. **Remove an element's attribute**:

```
let button = document.getElementById("changeText");
button.removeAttribute("disabled"); // Enable the button again
```

6. **Create a new element**:

```
let newParagraph = document.createElement("p");
newParagraph.textContent = "This is a new paragraph.";
document.body.appendChild(newParagraph); // Add the new paragraph to
the page
```

Real-World Example: Interacting with the DOM

Here's an example where we create an interactive webpage with a button to change text content dynamically. This demonstrates selecting, modifying, and interacting with elements in the DOM.

```
<!DOCTYPE html>
<html>
<head>
    <title>DOM Interaction Example</title>
</head>
<body>
    <h1>Click the button to change the heading text</h1>
    <button id="changeTextBtn">Change Text</button>

    <script>
        // Select the button and heading
        let button = document.getElementById("changeTextBtn");
        let heading = document.querySelector("h1");

        // Define the event handler
        function changeHeadingText() {
            heading.textContent = "The text has been changed!";
```

```
            heading.style.color = "green"; // Change the heading text color
        }

        // Attach the event listener to the button
        button.addEventListener("click", changeHeadingText);
    </script>
</body>
</html>
```

- When the user clicks the button, the `changeHeadingText` function is triggered.
- This function changes the content of the `<h1>` tag to "The text has been changed!" and updates the text color to green.

Selecting and Modifying Elements

In web development, manipulating HTML elements dynamically using JavaScript is essential for creating interactive, responsive websites. This interaction is possible through **DOM manipulation**, which includes selecting elements and modifying their properties (content, style, or attributes). In this explanation, we'll dive deeper into the methods used to **select** and **modify** DOM elements and provide more detailed examples.

Methods to Select Elements

There are various methods to select elements in the DOM. These methods can be used to target specific HTML tags, classes, or IDs, and even complex selectors similar to CSS queries.

1. getElementById:

The `getElementById` method selects an element by its unique **id** attribute. Since `id` values are required to be unique within a document, this method is ideal for selecting a specific element.

- **Usage**:

  ```
  let intro = document.getElementById('intro');
  console.log(intro);   // <p id="intro">This is an introduction
  paragraph.</p>
  ```

- **Explanation**:
  o `document.getElementById('intro')` targets the element with the `id="intro"`.
  o The method returns the first matching element, or `null` if no element with the specified ID is found.
- **Example**:

  ```
  <p id="intro">This is an introduction paragraph.</p>
  <script>
    let intro = document.getElementById('intro');
    intro.textContent = "This paragraph has been updated!";
  </script>
  ```

2. getElementsByClassName:

This method selects all elements with a specific class name. It returns an **HTMLCollection**, which is an array-like object. While you can access the elements by their index, you cannot directly use array methods like `map()` or `forEach()` without converting the collection to an actual array.

- **Usage**:

```
let paragraphs = document.getElementsByClassName('text');
console.log(paragraphs);  // HTMLCollection of elements with class
"text"
```

- **Example**:

```
<p class="text">First paragraph.</p>
<p class="text">Second paragraph.</p>
<script>
  let paragraphs = document.getElementsByClassName('text');
  for (let i = 0; i < paragraphs.length; i++) {
    paragraphs[i].textContent = "This is updated paragraph " + (i + 1);
  }
</script>
```

3. getElementsByTagName:

The `getElementsByTagName` method selects all elements of a specific tag name. Like `getElementsByClassName`, it returns an **HTMLCollection**.

- **Usage**:

```
let allDivs = document.getElementsByTagName('div');
console.log(allDivs);  // HTMLCollection of <div> elements
```

- **Example**:

```
<div>First div</div>
<div>Second div</div>
<script>
  let divs = document.getElementsByTagName('div');
  divs[0].textContent = "This is the first div!";
</script>
```

4. querySelector:

The `querySelector` method selects the **first element** that matches a CSS selector. It is more flexible than the previous methods, as it supports complex selectors (e.g., classes, ids, tag names, descendant selectors).

- **Usage**:

```javascript
let firstParagraph = document.querySelector('p');
console.log(firstParagraph);  // The first <p> element
```

- **Example**:

```html
<p>This is the first paragraph.</p>
<p>This is the second paragraph.</p>
<script>
  let firstParagraph = document.querySelector('p');
  firstParagraph.textContent = "The first paragraph has been changed!";
</script>
```

5. querySelectorAll:

querySelectorAll selects **all elements** that match a specified CSS selector and returns a **NodeList**. Unlike HTMLCollection, a NodeList is a true array-like object and can be iterated using array methods like forEach().

- **Usage**:

```javascript
let allParagraphs = document.querySelectorAll('p');
console.log(allParagraphs);  // NodeList of all <p> elements
```

- **Example**:

```html
<p>This is the first paragraph.</p>
<p>This is the second paragraph.</p>
<script>
  let paragraphs = document.querySelectorAll('p');
  paragraphs.forEach((para, index) => {
    para.textContent = "Updated paragraph " + (index + 1);
  });
</script>
```

Modifying Elements

Once elements are selected, you can modify their **content**, **attributes**, and **style** to dynamically update the page. Let's go over different ways to modify elements.

1. Change Text Content:

To modify the **text content** of an element, you can use the textContent property. It replaces the text inside the element and ensures no HTML tags are treated as part of the content.

- **Usage**:

```javascript
let intro = document.getElementById('intro');
intro.textContent = "This is a new introductory text.";
```

- **Explanation**:
  - o `textContent` updates the inner text of the element.
  - o Any existing text will be replaced with the new text.
- **Example**:

```
<p id="intro">This is an introduction paragraph.</p>
<script>
  let intro = document.getElementById('intro');
  intro.textContent = "This is a new introductory text.";
</script>
```

2. Change HTML Content:

If you want to change the **HTML structure** (including tags), you can use the `innerHTML` property. It allows you to inject HTML markup inside an element.

- **Usage**:

```
let intro = document.getElementById('intro');
intro.innerHTML = "<b>New bold introduction</b>";
```

- **Explanation**:
  - o `innerHTML` allows both text and HTML tags to be inserted.
  - o It can be useful when adding HTML elements dynamically but should be used carefully to avoid potential security risks like **XSS (Cross-Site Scripting)**.
- **Example**:

```
<p id="intro">This is an introduction paragraph.</p>
<script>
  let intro = document.getElementById('intro');
  intro.innerHTML = "<b>New bold introduction</b>";
</script>
```

3. Change an Attribute:

You can modify an element's **attributes** using the `setAttribute()` method. This allows you to change properties like `src`, `href`, `id`, `class`, etc.

- **Usage**:

```
let button = document.getElementById('changeText');
button.setAttribute('disabled', 'true'); // Disable the button
```

- **Explanation**:
  - o `setAttribute()` changes or adds an attribute to the selected element.
  - o In the example, we set the `disabled` attribute to `true`, which disables the button.
- **Example**:

```
<button id="changeText">Change Text</button>
<script>
  let button = document.getElementById('changeText');
```

```
  button.setAttribute('disabled', 'true');
</script>
```
4. Change Style:

To change the **style** of an element, you can directly modify the `style` property. This property gives access to the inline CSS styles of the element.

- **Usage**:

```
let h1 = document.querySelector('h1');
h1.style.color = 'red'; // Change the text color to red
```

- **Explanation**:
  - `style` modifies inline CSS for the selected element.
  - You can set CSS properties like `color`, `fontSize`, `backgroundColor`, etc.
- **Example**:

```
<h1>Welcome to my website</h1>
<script>
  let h1 = document.querySelector('h1');
  h1.style.color = 'red';  // Changes text color to red
  h1.style.fontSize = '30px'; // Changes font size to 30px
</script>
```

Event Handling and Listeners

Event handling is an essential concept in web development, allowing you to create interactive and dynamic websites. It enables you to define specific behaviors that happen in response to user actions or other events, such as clicking a button, moving the mouse over an element, or typing in a text field.

The core idea of event handling is that **events** are triggered when certain actions occur on HTML elements, and you can define a function, called an **event handler**, that will execute in response to that event.

Steps in Event Handling

There are two primary steps in event handling:

1. **Attach an Event Listener to an Element**: This step involves specifying which element will trigger the event and which event will trigger it (e.g., `click`, `mouseover`, `keydown`).
2. **Define the Event Handler**: This is the function that will execute when the event is triggered. It defines what happens after the event occurs.

Example: Button Click Event

Let's break down how we can set up an event handler on a button so that clicking it changes the text of an <h1> element:

```html
<!DOCTYPE html>
<html>
<head>
    <title>DOM Event Handling Example</title>
</head>
<body>
    <h1>Welcome to my website</h1>
    <button id="changeText">Change Text</button>

    <script>
        // Select the button
        let button = document.getElementById('changeText');

        // Define the event handler
        function changeText() {
            let heading = document.querySelector('h1');
            heading.textContent = "Text has been changed!";
        }

        // Attach the event listener
        button.addEventListener('click', changeText);
    </script>
</body>
</html>
```

How It Works:

- **Step 1 (Attach Event Listener)**:
  o The `addEventListener()` method is used to attach the event listener to the button. It listens for a `'click'` event.
  o When the button is clicked, the `changeText` function is called.
- **Step 2 (Event Handler)**:
  o The `changeText` function finds the <h1> element using `document.querySelector('h1')` and changes its text content to `"Text has been changed!"`.

Event Types

There are many types of events that you can listen for, and each type corresponds to a specific user action or event on the web page. Some of the common event types include:

- `click`: Triggered when an element is clicked (e.g., clicking a button or link).
- `mouseover`: Triggered when the mouse pointer enters an element (e.g., hovering over a button).
- `keydown`: Triggered when a key is pressed down (e.g., when a user types in a text input).

- **input**: Triggered when the value of an `<input>` or `<textarea>` element changes (e.g., typing in a text field).
- **submit**: Triggered when a form is submitted (e.g., clicking a "submit" button in a form).

Example of Multiple Event Listeners

You can attach multiple event listeners to a single element to make it respond to various actions. Here's an example where a button triggers two different actions—one when clicked and another when hovered over:

```
let button = document.getElementById('changeText');

// Click event listener
button.addEventListener('click', function() {
    alert('You clicked the button!');
});

// Mouseover event listener
button.addEventListener('mouseover', function() {
    console.log('Mouse is over the button!');
});
```

How It Works:

- The button has two event listeners:
    - The first listener listens for a `'click'` event, and when the button is clicked, an alert is displayed.
    - The second listener listens for a `'mouseover'` event, and when the mouse hovers over the button, a message is logged to the console.

Removing Event Listeners

In some cases, you may want to remove an event listener. This can be done using the `removeEventListener()` method. It's important to note that you need to pass the exact same function reference to `removeEventListener()` that was used when adding the event listener.

Here's an example where we remove the event listener:

```
function onClickHandler() {
    console.log('Button clicked');
}

let button = document.getElementById('changeText');

// Attach the event listener
button.addEventListener('click', onClickHandler);

// Later on, remove the event listener
button.removeEventListener('click', onClickHandler);
```

- **Explanation**:
    - Initially, we attach the `onClickHandler` function as the event listener for the `click` event.
    - Later, we use `removeEventListener()` to remove the listener from the button, so the event will no longer trigger the handler when clicked.

Practical Example - Combining All Concepts

Now let's combine the event handling concepts into a more practical example. In this case, we have a button that changes both the text and the style of a heading when clicked.

```
<!DOCTYPE html>
<html>
<head>
    <title>Interactive DOM Example</title>
</head>
<body>
    <h1>Click the button to change text and style</h1>
    <button id="changeText">Change Text and Style</button>

    <script>
        // Select the button and heading
        let button = document.getElementById('changeText');
        let heading = document.querySelector('h1');

        // Define the event handler
        function changeTextAndStyle() {
            heading.textContent = "The text has been changed!";
            heading.style.color = 'green'; // Change text color to green
        }

        // Attach the event listener
        button.addEventListener('click', changeTextAndStyle);
    </script>
</body>
</html>
```

How It Works:

1. **Button Selection**: We select the button using `document.getElementById('changeText')` and the heading using `document.querySelector('h1')`.
2. **Event Handler**: The `changeTextAndStyle` function updates the text content of the heading and changes its color to green.
3. **Event Listener**: The `addEventListener()` method is used to attach the `changeTextAndStyle` function to the button, so that when the button is clicked, the event handler is triggered.

Key Concepts of Event Handling:

- **Event Listener**: A function that "listens" for specific events (like click or keypress) on an element.
- **Event Handler**: A function that is executed when a specified event occurs.
- **Event Propagation**: By default, events "bubble" up through the DOM, meaning that the event can be handled at multiple levels (e.g., a click on a button can also trigger a click handler on the document). You can stop this propagation if needed using `event.stopPropagation()`.
- **Event Object**: When an event occurs, an event object is automatically passed to the event handler. This object contains information about the event, like the type of event, the target element, and more.

Conclusion

1. **DOM** is the structure that represents the HTML or XML document and allows dynamic interaction.
2. **Selecting Elements** in the DOM is done using various methods like `getElementById`, `getElementsByClassName`, and `querySelector`.
3. **Event Handling** allows us to specify actions (functions) that should happen when specific events (like clicks or keypresses) occur on elements.
4. By **modifying the DOM** dynamically, you can create interactive and responsive web pages.

25 multiple-choice questions (MCQs) covering the topics of the DOM (Document Object Model), Selecting and Modifying Elements, and Event Handling and Listeners:

Understanding the DOM (Document Object Model)

1. **What does the DOM represent?** a) Only the structure of a webpage
   b) The entire webpage content as an object
   c) Only the styles of a webpage
   d) Only the events on a webpage

   Answer: b) The entire webpage content as an object

2. **Which of the following is the root node in the DOM?** a) `<html>`
   b) `<body>`
   c) `<div>`
   d) `<head>`

   Answer: a) `<html>`

3. **Which of the following represents a text node in the DOM?** a) <div>
   b) An empty string
   c) The actual text content inside elements
   d) An empty element

   Answer: c) The actual text content inside elements

4. **Which method is used to select an element by its ID in JavaScript?** a)
   getElementsByTagName()
   b) querySelector()
   c) getElementById()
   d) querySelectorAll()

   Answer: c) getElementById()

5. **Which object in the DOM represents an entire webpage?** a) document
   b) body
   c) head
   d) html

   Answer: a) document

6. **What is an example of an attribute in the DOM?** a) Text content inside an element
   b) A class name
   c) The entire element itself
   d) The entire webpage

   Answer: b) A class name

7. **What does `document.querySelector('div')` do?** a) Selects the first <div> element in the document
   b) Selects all <div> elements in the document
   c) Selects the first element with a div class
   d) Selects the first <div> element in the body only

   Answer: a) Selects the first <div> element in the document

8. **What is the purpose of the `textContent` property in the DOM?** a) To modify the HTML inside an element
   b) To retrieve the text inside an element
   c) To add an event listener to an element
   d) To change the style of an element

   Answer: b) To retrieve the text inside an element

9. **Which DOM method is used to select all elements of a certain tag name?** a) `getElementById()`

    b) `getElementsByClassName()`

    c) `getElementsByTagName()`

    d) `querySelectorAll()`

    Answer: c) `getElementsByTagName()`

10. **Which of the following is NOT part of the DOM?** a) `<div>` element

    b) The content of a form

    c) The CSS styles applied to an element

    d) The HTML document itself

    Answer: c) The CSS styles applied to an element

Selecting and Modifying Elements

11. **How do you select all elements with a class of `example` in JavaScript?** a) `document.querySelector('example')`

    b) `document.querySelectorAll('.example')`

    c) `document.getElementsByClassName('example')`

    d) `document.getElementsByTagName('example')`

    Answer: b) `document.querySelectorAll('.example')`

12. **What method is used to change the content inside an HTML element?** a) `textContent`

    b) `innerHTML`

    c) `style`

    d) `setAttribute()`

    Answer: b) `innerHTML`

13. **How can you modify the background color of an element using JavaScript?** a) `element.style.backgroundColor = 'red';`

    b) `element.style.background = 'red';`

    c) `element.setAttribute('style', 'background:red');`

    d) All of the above

    Answer: d) All of the above

14. **Which property is used to change the HTML attributes of an element?** a) `setAttribute()`

    b) `textContent`

    c) `innerHTML`

    d) `style`

    Answer: a) `setAttribute()`

15. **What does the `classList.add()` method do?** a) Adds a class to an element's class attribute

    b) Removes a class from an element's class attribute

    c) Changes the content of an element

    d) Modifies the inline style of an element

    Answer: a) Adds a class to an element's class attribute

16. **Which method will give you a list of all the `<p>` elements on a webpage?** a) `document.getElementByTagName('p')`

    b) `document.querySelectorAll('p')`

    c) `document.getElementsByClassName('p')`

    d) `document.querySelector('p')`

    Answer: b) `document.querySelectorAll('p')`

17. **How can you access an element's attribute in JavaScript?** a) `element.getAttribute('attributeName')`

    b) `element.setAttribute('attributeName')`

    c) `element.attributeName`

    d) `element.attributes['attributeName']`

    Answer: a) `element.getAttribute('attributeName')`

18. **What is the correct syntax to set the value of an `input` element in JavaScript?** a) `input.setValue('new value')`

    b) `input.setAttribute('value', 'new value')`

    c) `input.value = 'new value'`

    d) `input.innerHTML = 'new value'`

    Answer: c) `input.value = 'new value'`

Event Handling and Listeners

19. **Which method is used to attach an event listener to an element in JavaScript?** a) `addListener()`

    b) `addEvent()`

    c) `addEventListener()`

    d) `attachEvent()`

    Answer: c) `addEventListener()`

20. **Which event is triggered when a user clicks on an element?** a) `mouseover`

    b) `focus`

    c) `click`

    d) `input`

    Answer: c) `click`

21. **Which of the following is the correct way to remove an event listener?** a) `element.removeListener('click', myFunction)`

    b) `element.removeEventListener('click', myFunction)`

    c) `element.detachEventListener('click', myFunction)`

    d) `element.removeEvent('click', myFunction)`

    Answer: b) `element.removeEventListener('click', myFunction)`

22. **What is the purpose of the `event.preventDefault()` method?** a) To stop the propagation of the event

    b) To prevent the default action associated with the event

    c) To trigger another event

    d) To stop the event listener from being called

    Answer: b) To prevent the default action associated with the event

23. **Which event occurs when the user moves the mouse pointer over an element?** a) `click`

    b) `mouseover`

    c) `keydown`

    d) `focus`

    Answer: b) `mouseover`

24. **What is the correct way to define an anonymous function as an event handler?** a) `element.addEventListener('click', function() { /* code */ });`

    b) `element.addEventListener('click', new Function() { /* code */ });`

    c) `element.addEventListener('click', function() { return /* code */ });`

    d) `element.addEventListener('click', { /* code */ });`

Answer: a) `element.addEventListener('click', function() { /* code */ });`

25. **What happens when an event listener is attached to the document object?** a) It listens for events only on the body element
b) It listens for events on the entire document, including all elements
c) It listens for events only on the `html` element
d) It listens for events only on the `head` element

Answer: b) It listens for events on the entire document, including all elements

CHAPTER-7

JAVASCRIPT IN WEB DEVELOPMENT

Integrating JavaScript with HTML and CSS

Integrating JavaScript with HTML and CSS allows you to make web pages dynamic and interactive. JavaScript interacts with HTML to manipulate the page's content and structure and with CSS to modify the styles of elements in real-time. This integration creates an engaging experience for users as the page responds to user interactions.

1. Integrating JavaScript with HTML

HTML provides the structure of a webpage (e.g., headings, paragraphs, images, buttons). JavaScript allows you to enhance this structure by adding dynamic behavior and interactivity. You can integrate JavaScript into HTML in three main ways:

1.1 Inline JavaScript

Inline JavaScript is written directly in the HTML element's attribute, typically within event handlers such as `onclick`, `onmouseover`, `onkeyup`, etc. This method allows quick and simple integration but isn't ideal for complex functionality because it mixes HTML and JavaScript.

Example:

```
<!DOCTYPE html>
<html>
<head>
    <title>Inline JavaScript Example</title>
</head>
<body>
    <!-- Inline JavaScript that runs when the button is clicked -->
    <button onclick="alert('Hello, World!')">Click me</button>
</body>
</html>
```

- In this example, the `onclick` attribute directly triggers a JavaScript function (`alert()`) when the user clicks the button.
- The advantage is simplicity for small tasks, but this can quickly become difficult to maintain for large projects.

1.2 Internal JavaScript

Internal JavaScript is written within `<script>` tags in the `<head>` or `<body>` section of an HTML document. This method allows you to keep JavaScript code organized and separate from the HTML structure, while still being embedded in the same file.

Example:

```
<!DOCTYPE html>
<html>
<head>
    <title>Internal JavaScript Example</title>
    <script>
        // Define the JavaScript function
        function changeColor() {
            document.body.style.backgroundColor = "lightblue";  // Change the
background color
        }
    </script>
</head>
<body>
    <!-- Button that triggers the function when clicked -->
    <button onclick="changeColor()">Change Background Color</button>
</body>
</html>
```

- The `changeColor()` function is defined inside the `<script>` tag and changes the background color when the button is clicked.
- The script is placed in the `<head>` tag but can also be placed in the `<body>` for easier access to elements.

1.3 External JavaScript

External JavaScript is the most scalable and maintainable approach, especially for large projects. You write JavaScript code in a separate `.js` file and link to it in the HTML document using the `<script>` tag. This method keeps HTML clean and enables reusability of the same JavaScript code across multiple HTML files.

Example:

```
<!DOCTYPE html>
<html>
<head>
    <title>External JavaScript Example</title>
    <script src="script.js"></script>  <!-- Link to external JavaScript file
-->
</head>
<body>
    <button onclick="changeText()">Click me</button>
```

```
</body>
</html>
```

```
script.js:
```

```javascript
// External JavaScript function to change the button text
function changeText() {
    document.querySelector("button").textContent = "You clicked me!";
}
```

- In this example, `script.js` is an external JavaScript file that changes the text of the button when clicked.
- This approach promotes separation of concerns and is ideal for larger projects where the JavaScript logic is complex.

2. Integrating JavaScript with CSS

JavaScript can manipulate the CSS of HTML elements dynamically, enabling real-time changes based on user interactions. You can modify CSS properties directly or add/remove CSS classes to apply predefined styles.

2.1 Changing Styles Using JavaScript

You can use JavaScript to change the inline styles of an HTML element. This is done through the `style` property, which allows direct manipulation of CSS properties.

Example:

```html
<!DOCTYPE html>
<html>
<head>
    <title>Change CSS with JavaScript</title>
</head>
<body>
    <button onclick="changeStyle()">Change Style</button>

    <script>
        function changeStyle() {
            // Dynamically change the background color and font family
            document.body.style.backgroundColor = "yellow";   // Change
background color
            document.body.style.fontFamily = "Arial, sans-serif";  // Change
font style
        }
    </script>
</body>
</html>
```

- When the button is clicked, the `changeStyle()` function changes the background color to yellow and the font to Arial.
- The `style` property is a direct way to apply individual CSS properties, but for more complex or reusable styles, adding/removing CSS classes is preferred.

2.2 Adding or Removing CSS Classes

Instead of directly changing inline styles, JavaScript can add or remove CSS classes to elements. This method is preferred for maintaining reusable styles and keeping HTML and CSS separate. By toggling classes, you can apply predefined styles to elements.

Example:

```
<!DOCTYPE html>
<html>
<head>
    <title>Add Class with JavaScript</title>
    <style>
        /* Define a class that highlights an element */
        .highlight {
            background-color: yellow;
            color: red;
        }
    </style>
</head>
<body>
    <button id="myButton">Click me to highlight</button>

    <script>
        // Add 'highlight' class to the button when it's clicked
        document.getElementById("myButton").onclick = function() {
            this.classList.add("highlight");  // Add the highlight class
        }
    </script>
</body>
</html>
```

- In this example, the button gains the `.highlight` class when clicked, changing its background to yellow and the text color to red.
- The `classList.add()` method is used to add the class, which allows you to manage styles through CSS classes instead of inline styles.

2.3 Removing CSS Classes

You can also remove CSS classes dynamically using JavaScript. This is useful when you need to revert changes or toggle between different styles.

Example:

```
<!DOCTYPE html>
```

```html
<html>
<head>
    <title>Remove Class with JavaScript</title>
    <style>
        .highlight {
            background-color: yellow;
            color: red;
        }
    </style>
</head>
<body>
    <button id="toggleButton">Click me to toggle highlight</button>

    <script>
        // Toggle the highlight class when clicked
        document.getElementById("toggleButton").onclick = function() {
            this.classList.toggle("highlight");  // Toggle the class
        }
    </script>
</body>
</html>
```

- When the button is clicked, the `highlight` class is either added or removed from the button, depending on whether the class is currently applied.
- The `classList.toggle()` method is used to toggle the class, which is helpful for switching between styles.

Working with Forms in JavaScript

Forms are a core part of user interactions on the web. They allow users to input data that can be processed, validated, and sent to a server. JavaScript provides powerful capabilities for managing form submissions, performing client-side validation, and dynamically interacting with form elements. Below is a detailed explanation of how JavaScript integrates with forms to provide these features.

1. Handling Form Submission

Form submission is often triggered when a user clicks the submit button. JavaScript can intercept this submission to process the form data, prevent the page from reloading, or send the data asynchronously without refreshing the page (using technologies like AJAX).

1.1 Preventing Default Form Submission

By default, when a form is submitted, the page reloads, and the form data is sent to the server. However, you may want to handle the submission yourself (e.g., validate the form or send it via

JavaScript). In such cases, you can prevent the default form submission behavior using `event.preventDefault()`.

Example:

```html
<!DOCTYPE html>
<html>
<head>
    <title>Form Submission Example</title>
</head>
<body>
    <form id="myForm">
        <input type="text" id="username" placeholder="Enter username">
        <input type="password" id="password" placeholder="Enter password">
        <button type="submit">Submit</button>
    </form>

    <script>
        // Attach event listener to the form
        document.getElementById("myForm").addEventListener("submit",
function(event) {
            event.preventDefault();  // Prevent the default form submission

            // Capture form values
            let username = document.getElementById("username").value;
            let password = document.getElementById("password").value;

            // Log the form data (or process it further)
            console.log("Username:", username);
            console.log("Password:", password);
        });
    </script>
</body>
</html>
```

- **How it works:**
  - The `submit` event listener intercepts the form submission.
  - The `event.preventDefault()` method prevents the form from submitting in the default way (i.e., refreshing the page).
  - JavaScript captures the values entered in the input fields, which can be processed, validated, or sent to a server.
- **Use Case:**
  - This is often used when submitting data asynchronously (e.g., via AJAX) without reloading the page.

---

2. Validating Form Inputs

Form validation ensures that the data entered by the user meets the required criteria before submission. JavaScript can be used to perform client-side validation, helping to ensure that the data is correct and complete before being submitted to the server.

2.1 Basic Input Validation

In simple form validation, you might check for empty fields, incorrect formats (e.g., email or phone number), or specific rules (e.g., password length). JavaScript allows you to validate these conditions before the form is submitted.

Example:

```
<!DOCTYPE html>
<html>
<head>
    <title>Form Validation</title>
</head>
<body>
    <form id="registrationForm">
        <input type="email" id="email" placeholder="Enter your email"
required>
        <input type="password" id="password" placeholder="Enter your
password" required>
        <button type="submit">Register</button>
    </form>

    <script>
        // Add event listener for form submission
document.getElementById("registrationForm").addEventListener("submit",
function(event) {
            let email = document.getElementById("email").value;
            let password = document.getElementById("password").value;

            // Basic validation: Check if email and password are provided
            if (email === "" || password === "") {
                alert("Please fill in all fields.");
                event.preventDefault();  // Prevent form submission if fields
are empty
            } else if (!email.includes("@")) {  // Simple email validation
                alert("Please enter a valid email.");
                event.preventDefault();  // Prevent form submission if email
is invalid
            }
        });
    </script>
</body>
</html>
```

- **How it works:**
    - The form is intercepted when the user submits it.
    - JavaScript checks if the email and password fields are empty.
    - If the email does not contain the @ symbol, the form is not submitted, and an alert is displayed to the user.
    - The `event.preventDefault()` method is used to prevent the form from being submitted if validation fails.
- **Use Case:**

- This is commonly used for basic validation where the form shouldn't submit unless the input is correct.

2.2 Advanced Validation (Regex and Custom Rules)

Sometimes, more complex validation is required, such as ensuring that an email address follows a specific pattern or checking that the password meets certain criteria (e.g., minimum length, contains numbers, etc.). JavaScript can utilize Regular Expressions (regex) for these validations.

Example (Advanced Email and Password Validation):

```
<!DOCTYPE html>
<html>
<head>
    <title>Advanced Form Validation</title>
</head>
<body>
    <form id="loginForm">
        <input type="email" id="email" placeholder="Enter your email"
required>
        <input type="password" id="password" placeholder="Enter your
password" required>
        <button type="submit">Login</button>
    </form>

    <script>
        document.getElementById("loginForm").addEventListener("submit",
function(event) {
            let email = document.getElementById("email").value;
            let password = document.getElementById("password").value;

            // Email Validation (Regex pattern)
            const emailPattern = /^[a-zA-Z0-9._-]+@[a-zA-Z0-9.-]+\.[a-zA-
Z]{2,6}$/;
            if (!emailPattern.test(email)) {
                alert("Please enter a valid email.");
                event.preventDefault();  // Prevent form submission
                return;  // Stop further validation
            }

            // Password Validation (at least 6 characters)
            if (password.length < 6) {
                alert("Password must be at least 6 characters long.");
                event.preventDefault();  // Prevent form submission
            }
        });
    </script>
</body>
</html>
```

- **How it works:**
  - A Regular Expression (`emailPattern`) is used to validate that the email matches a typical email format.

- o A simple password length check ensures that the password is at least 6 characters long.
- o If validation fails, an alert is shown and the form submission is prevented.

3. Dynamically Updating Form Elements

JavaScript provides a powerful way to dynamically interact with form elements. This allows developers to create more interactive and user-friendly forms that can adapt based on the user's actions. Some common dynamic interactions include enabling or disabling form elements, updating placeholder text, and modifying the visibility of certain form fields.

3.1 Enabling/Disabling Form Elements

One common use of JavaScript in forms is to enable or disable form elements based on certain conditions. This ensures that users only interact with fields when necessary, or prevents form submission if certain criteria are not met.

Example: Disabling Submit Button Until All Fields Are Filled

In this example, we use JavaScript to ensure the user has entered values in all required fields before the submit button becomes active. If one of the fields is left empty, the submit button remains disabled.

HTML:

```
<!DOCTYPE html>
<html>
<head>
    <title>Dynamic Form Example</title>
</head>
<body>
    <form id="dynamicForm">
        <input type="text" id="username" placeholder="Enter your username"
required>
        <input type="password" id="password" placeholder="Enter your
password" required>
        <button type="submit" id="submitButton" disabled>Submit</button>
    </form>

    <script>
        // Listen for input changes on the form
        document.getElementById("dynamicForm").addEventListener("input",
function() {
            let username = document.getElementById("username").value;
            let password = document.getElementById("password").value;
            let submitButton = document.getElementById("submitButton");
```

```
                // Enable button if both fields are filled
                if (username && password) {
                    submitButton.disabled = false;   // Enable the submit button
                } else {
                    submitButton.disabled = true;    // Keep the button disabled
                }
            });
    </script>
</body>
</html>
```

How it Works:

- The JavaScript listens for `input` events on the form, which is triggered whenever the user types into the input fields.
- It checks if both the username and password fields are non-empty.
- If both fields are filled, the submit button is enabled (`submitButton.disabled = false`).
- If either field is empty, the submit button remains disabled (`submitButton.disabled = true`).

Use Cases:

- **Forms with required fields:** You can prevent the user from submitting a form if required fields are missing.
- **Step-by-step form submission:** Use dynamic enabling/disabling to guide the user through a form's multi-step process.

3.2 Other Dynamic Interactions with Form Elements

Beyond just enabling and disabling fields, JavaScript can be used to modify form behavior based on user input. This includes changing form field attributes (such as placeholder text), hiding/showing certain form sections, or even altering form field types.

Example 1: Changing Placeholder Text Based on User Input

In this example, the placeholder text of an input field changes dynamically based on the value entered in another field.

HTML:

```
<!DOCTYPE html>
<html>
<head>
    <title>Dynamic Placeholder Example</title>
</head>
<body>
    <form id="dynamicForm">
        <input type="text" id="username" placeholder="Enter your username"
required>
```

```
        <input type="email" id="email" placeholder="Enter your email"
required>
        <button type="submit" id="submitButton">Submit</button>
    </form>

    <script>
        document.getElementById("username").addEventListener("input",
function() {
            let username = document.getElementById("username").value;
            let emailField = document.getElementById("email");

            // Change email placeholder text based on username input
            if (username.length > 0) {
                emailField.placeholder = "Enter your email for " + username;
            } else {
                emailField.placeholder = "Enter your email";
            }
        });
    </script>
</body>
</html>
```

How it Works:

- When the user types in the `username` input field, the placeholder text of the `email` input field updates based on the username.
- If the `username` field is empty, the placeholder reverts to the default message.

Use Cases:

- **Personalized forms:** You can customize placeholders to provide a more personalized experience.
- **Context-sensitive input:** The form can provide guidance or hints specific to the user's input.

3.3 Show/Hide Form Elements Based on User Input

Another common feature is to show or hide form elements dynamically based on certain conditions. For example, you might show additional fields if a user selects a particular option in a dropdown menu, or reveal additional information when a checkbox is checked.

Example: Show Additional Fields Based on Checkbox Selection

In this example, a checkbox is used to reveal additional fields only if the checkbox is checked.

HTML:

```
<!DOCTYPE html>
<html>
<head>
```

```html
    <title>Show/Hide Fields Example</title>
</head>
<body>
    <form id="dynamicForm">
        <label>
            <input type="checkbox" id="newsletter" name="newsletter">
Subscribe to newsletter
        </label>
        <br>

        <div id="additionalFields" style="display: none;">
            <input type="text" id="email" placeholder="Enter your email">
            <input type="text" id="preferences" placeholder="Enter your
preferences">
        </div>

        <button type="submit" id="submitButton">Submit</button>
    </form>

    <script>
        document.getElementById("newsletter").addEventListener("change",
function() {
            let additionalFields =
document.getElementById("additionalFields");

            // Show or hide additional fields based on checkbox state
            if (this.checked) {
                additionalFields.style.display = "block";  // Show additional
fields
            } else {
                additionalFields.style.display = "none";   // Hide additional
fields
            }
        });
    </script>
</body>
</html>
```

How it Works:

- The `newsletter` checkbox is monitored for changes (`change` event).
- When the checkbox is checked, the `additionalFields` section is shown by setting its `display` style to `"block"`.
- When the checkbox is unchecked, the `additionalFields` section is hidden by setting its `display` style to `"none"`.

Use Cases:

- **Conditional inputs:** Only show fields that are necessary based on user preferences or selections.
- **Dynamic forms:** Make the form responsive by showing/hiding sections as the user interacts with it.

Using JavaScript with External APIs

External APIs allow you to fetch data from third-party services or send data to remote servers. JavaScript is commonly used to interact with these APIs through `fetch()` requests. Below are examples of using `fetch()` to get data and send data to APIs.

---

1. Fetching Data from an External API

The `fetch()` method is used to make asynchronous HTTP requests. It can retrieve data from an API and update the webpage dynamically without requiring a page reload.

Example: Fetching a Random Dog Image

In this example, when the user clicks a button, a random dog image is fetched from the Dog CEO API and displayed on the webpage.

HTML:

```html
<!DOCTYPE html>
<html>
<head>
    <title>Fetch API Example</title>
</head>
<body>
    <h1>Random Dog Image</h1>
    <button onclick="getRandomDog()">Get Dog Image</button>
    <img id="dogImage" src="" alt="Random Dog" style="width: 300px; height:
auto;">

    <script>
        function getRandomDog() {
            fetch("https://dog.ceo/api/breeds/image/random")
                .then(response => response.json())
                .then(data => {
                    document.getElementById("dogImage").src = data.message;
// Display the dog image
                })
                .catch(error => console.error("Error fetching dog image:",
error));
        }
    </script>
</body>
</html>
```

How it Works:

- When the button is clicked, the `getRandomDog()` function is called.
- The `fetch()` function makes a GET request to the Dog CEO API to retrieve a random dog image.
- The image URL is then dynamically inserted into the `src` attribute of the `<img>` tag.

Use Cases:

- **Displaying live data:** Fetching data from external services like weather, news, or social media.
- **Interactive features:** Use external APIs to provide dynamic content, such as random jokes, quotes, or images.

---

2. Sending Data with a POST Request

In addition to fetching data, you can use JavaScript to send data to external APIs, such as submitting a form.

Example: Sending Form Data with POST

In this example, form data is sent to a fictional server API using a POST request.

HTML:

```
<!DOCTYPE html>
<html>
<head>
    <title>POST Data to API</title>
</head>
<body>
    <h1>Submit Data to Server</h1>
    <form id="dataForm">
        <input type="text" id="name" placeholder="Enter your name">
        <input type="email" id="email" placeholder="Enter your email">
        <button type="submit">Submit</button>
    </form>

    <script>
        document.getElementById("dataForm").addEventListener("submit",
function(event) {
            event.preventDefault(); // Prevent form submission
            const name = document.getElementById("name").value;
            const email = document.getElementById("email").value;

            fetch('https://example.com/api/submit', {
                method: 'POST',
                headers: {
                    'Content-Type': 'application/json'
                },
                body: JSON.stringify({ name, email })  // Send form data as
JSON
            })
            .then(response => response.json())
            .then(data => console.log("Server response:", data))
            .catch(error => console.error("Error:", error));
        });
    </script>
```

```
</body>
</html>
```
How it Works:

- The form data (name and email) is sent to the server API using a POST request.
- The `fetch()` function includes a `body` property that sends the data as a JSON string.
- The response from the server is processed asynchronously and logged to the console.

Use Cases:

- **Form submission to a server:** Submitting user input to a database or server-side application.
- **Async data processing:** Sending form data without refreshing the page.

Conclusion

JavaScript plays a crucial role in integrating HTML and CSS to create interactive, dynamic web applications. You can:

- Dynamically modify HTML content and apply CSS styles.
- Handle form submissions, validate inputs, and send or receive data from external APIs.
- Use the `fetch()` API to interact with external services, enabling real-time data updates on your webpage.

25 multiple-choice questions (MCQs) based on the topics "Integrating JavaScript with HTML and CSS," "Working with Forms," and "Using JavaScript with External APIs."

Integrating JavaScript with HTML and CSS

1. **Which of the following is the correct way to link an external JavaScript file to an HTML document?**
   - A) `<script href="script.js"></script>`
   - B) `<link href="script.js"></link>`
   - C) `<script src="script.js"></script>`
   - D) `<script ref="script.js"></script>`

   Answer: C) `<script src="script.js"></script>`

2. **Where is the JavaScript code generally placed in an HTML document to ensure it works properly?**
   - A) Inside `<head>` tag only
   - B) Inside `<body>` tag only
   - C) Inside the `<script>` tag, either in `<head>` or `<body>`

o D) Inside `<html>` tag only

Answer: C) Inside the `<script>` tag, either in `<head>` or `<body>`

3. **How can you change the background color of a webpage using JavaScript?**
   - o A) `document.body.style.backgroundColor = 'blue';`
   - o B) `document.body.style.color = 'blue';`
   - o C) `document.style.backgroundColor = 'blue';`
   - o D) `document.body.backgroundColor = 'blue';`

Answer: A) `document.body.style.backgroundColor = 'blue';`

4. **What does the following JavaScript code do?**

```
document.getElementById("myButton").onclick = function() {
    alert("Button clicked!");
}
```

   - o A) Changes the button text
   - o B) Creates a new button
   - o C) Displays an alert when the button is clicked
   - o D) Adds a click event to all buttons

Answer: C) Displays an alert when the button is clicked

5. **Which of the following is true when using JavaScript to manipulate HTML elements?**
   - o A) You cannot modify the content of an HTML element
   - o B) JavaScript can only modify CSS styles
   - o C) JavaScript can modify both HTML content and CSS styles dynamically
   - o D) JavaScript can only read HTML content

Answer: C) JavaScript can modify both HTML content and CSS styles dynamically

6. **How do you add a CSS class to an element using JavaScript?**
   - o A) `element.style.className = "newClass";`
   - o B) `element.addClass("newClass");`
   - o C) `element.classList.add("newClass");`
   - o D) `element.className = "newClass";`

Answer: C) `element.classList.add("newClass");`

Working with Forms

7. **Which of the following methods is used to prevent the default form submission behavior in JavaScript?**
   - o A) `event.preventSubmit();`
   - o B) `event.preventDefault();`
   - o C) `event.stopPropagation();`
   - o D) `event.stopSubmit();`

   Answer: B) `event.preventDefault();`

8. **How do you capture the value of an input field with the id "username" in JavaScript?**
   - o A) `document.getElementById("username").value;`
   - o B) `document.getElementById("username").textContent;`
   - o C) `document.getElementById("username").innerHTML;`
   - o D) `document.querySelector("username").value;`

   Answer: A) `document.getElementById("username").value;`

9. **How do you validate an email field using JavaScript to ensure it contains "@"?**
   - o A) `if (email.indexOf("@") != -1) { }`
   - o B) `if (email.includes("@")) { }`
   - o C) `if (email.contains("@")) { }`
   - o D) `if (email.has("@")) { }`

   Answer: B) `if (email.includes("@")) { }`

10. **Which method is used to submit a form programmatically in JavaScript?**
    - o A) `form.submit();`
    - o B) `form.submitForm();`
    - o C) `form.triggerSubmit();`
    - o D) `form.send();`

    Answer: A) `form.submit();`

11. **How do you disable a submit button until both required fields are filled?**
    - o A) `document.getElementById("submit").disabled = true;`
    - o B) `document.getElementById("submit").disabled = false;`
    - o C) Use JavaScript to check field values and enable/disable the button
    - o D) All of the above

    Answer: C) Use JavaScript to check field values and enable/disable the button

12. **Which HTML attribute is used to make an input field required in a form?**
   - o A) `required`
   - o B) `mandatory`
   - o C) `mustfill`
   - o D) `validate`

   Answer: A) `required`

13. **What JavaScript function can you use to get the value of a checkbox?**
   - o A) `checkbox.checked()`
   - o B) `checkbox.isChecked()`
   - o C) `checkbox.checked`
   - o D) `checkbox.value()`

   Answer: C) `checkbox.checked`

14. **How do you dynamically change the placeholder text of an input field in JavaScript?**
   - o A) `input.placeholder = "New placeholder";`
   - o B) `input.placeholderText = "New placeholder";`
   - o C) `input.setAttribute("placeholder", "New placeholder");`
   - o D) `input.placeholder = "New placeholder";`

   Answer: A) `input.placeholder = "New placeholder";`

15. **What happens when you call `event.preventDefault()` in a form submission event handler?**
   - o A) It submits the form data
   - o B) It cancels the form submission
   - o C) It clears the form inputs
   - o D) It prevents the form from being displayed

   Answer: B) It cancels the form submission

Using JavaScript with External APIs

16. **Which method is commonly used to make HTTP requests to an API in JavaScript?**
   - o A) `fetch()`
   - o B) `ajax()`
   - o C) `request()`
   - o D) `httpRequest()`

   Answer: A) `fetch()`

17. **What does the `fetch()` function return in JavaScript?**
    - A) A Promise that resolves to the response object
    - B) A callback function
    - C) The server response directly
    - D) A string containing the response body

    Answer: A) A Promise that resolves to the response object

18. **Which of the following methods is used to convert the response from a fetch request into JSON?**
    - A) `response.toJson();`
    - B) `response.json();`
    - C) `response.parseJson();`
    - D) `response.text();`

    Answer: B) `response.json();`

19. **Which of the following is true about using `fetch()` with the `POST` method?**
    - A) You can only send GET requests with `fetch()`
    - B) `fetch()` does not allow sending data to an API
    - C) You use the `method: 'POST'` option to send data
    - D) `fetch()` automatically sends data with GET requests

    Answer: C) You use the `method: 'POST'` option to send data

20. **How do you handle errors when using the `fetch()` function?**
    - A) Use `.catch()` to catch any errors
    - B) Use `try...catch` around the fetch call
    - C) Both A and B
    - D) Errors in `fetch()` cannot be handled

    Answer: C) Both A and B

21. **What is the correct format to send data to a server in a `POST` request using `fetch()`?**
    - A) `body: "name=John&email=john@example.com"`
    - B) `body: { name: "John", email: "john@example.com" }`
    - C) `body: JSON.stringify({ name: "John", email: "john@example.com" })`
    - D) `body: { name: "John", email: "john@example.com" }`

    Answer: C) `body: JSON.stringify({ name: "John", email:`

    `"john@example.com" })`

22. **What does the `then()` method do in the context of a `fetch()` request?**
    - o A) Handles the response after the request completes
    - o B) Sends data to the server
    - o C) Starts a new request
    - o D) It is used to handle form data submission

    Answer: A) Handles the response after the request completes

23. **Which HTTP method is used by default in a `fetch()` request?**
    - o A) POST
    - o B) GET
    - o C) PUT
    - o D) DELETE

    Answer: B) GET

24. **How can you display the data returned from an API call in the DOM?**
    - o A) `document.body.innerHTML = data;`
    - o B) `document.getElementById("id").innerText = data;`
    - o C) `document.write(data);`
    - o D) All of the above

    Answer: D) All of the above

25. **What is the correct way to handle asynchronous operations when using `fetch()` in JavaScript?**
    - o A) Use `async/await`
    - o B) Use `.then()` for promise chaining
    - o C) Both A and B
    - o D) Asynchronous operations cannot be used with `fetch()`

    Answer: C) Both A and B

CHAPTER-8

Writing Clean and Readable Code

Writing clean and readable code is critical for maintaining a well-structured codebase, especially in collaborative projects or when dealing with long-term maintenance. Clean code improves readability, reduces bugs, and allows developers to easily add new features or fix issues without introducing errors.

Here are **detailed guidelines** to help write clean and readable JavaScript code, along with practical examples:

---

1. Use Descriptive Variable and Function Names

The purpose of naming variables and functions is to communicate their role or what they represent. Meaningful names prevent ambiguity and make the code easier to read and understand.

Guidelines:

- Avoid one-letter variable names, except for loop counters.
- Use names that describe the purpose of the variable or the action the function performs.
- Use consistent naming conventions, such as camelCase for variables and functions, PascalCase for classes, and UPPERCASE for constants.

Example:
```
// Bad practice
let a = 5;
let b = 10;
let c = a + b;

// Good practice
let totalPrice = 5;
let discountPrice = 10;
let finalPrice = totalPrice + discountPrice;
```

Explanation:

- `a`, `b`, and `c` do not explain what they represent. In contrast, `totalPrice`, `discountPrice`, and `finalPrice` clearly communicate their meanings.
- Clear naming helps future developers understand the intent of the code at a glance.

---

2. Follow Consistent Indentation and Spacing

Indentation ensures that the code is properly structured, making it easy to read and understand. Consistency in spacing makes the code uniform and visually clean.

Guidelines:

- Use 2 or 4 spaces for indentation (pick one and stick to it).
- Use blank lines to separate logically distinct code blocks, such as functions or conditionals.

Example:
```
// Bad practice
function calculatePrice(price, discount) {
    let finalPrice=price - discount; return finalPrice;
}

// Good practice
function calculatePrice(price, discount) {
    let finalPrice = price - discount;
    return finalPrice;
}
```

Explanation:

- In the "Bad practice" example, everything is written on one line, making it difficult to read.
- The "Good practice" example separates the logic into different lines, with proper indentation, making it easier to follow.

---

3. Avoid Magic Numbers

Magic numbers are arbitrary values that appear in the code without context, which makes the code harder to understand. These numbers should be replaced with named constants or variables that clarify their meaning.

Guidelines:

- Replace hardcoded numbers with constants or variables that have descriptive names.

Example:

```
// Bad practice
let area = length * 3.1416 * radius * radius; // 3.1416 is a "magic number"

// Good practice
const PI = 3.1416;
let area = length * PI * radius * radius;
```

Explanation:

- The number 3.1416 in the "Bad practice" example is unclear and requires knowledge of its significance.
- By defining PI as a constant, the code in the "Good practice" example is more self-explanatory and maintainable.

4. Write Small Functions

A function should do one thing and do it well. Smaller, focused functions are easier to read, test, and maintain. Large, complex functions tend to be error-prone and hard to manage.

Guidelines:

- A function should have a single responsibility.
- If a function does too many things, break it into smaller, more manageable parts.

Example:
```
// Bad practice
function processOrder(order) {
    // Validate the order
    // Calculate discount
    // Process payment
    // Generate invoice
}

// Good practice
function validateOrder(order) {
    // Validate the order
}

function calculateDiscount(order) {
    // Calculate discount
}

function processPayment(order) {
    // Process payment
}

function generateInvoice(order) {
    // Generate invoice
}
```

Explanation:

- In the "Bad practice" example, the function processOrder handles multiple tasks.
- In the "Good practice" example, each function has one clear responsibility, making the code easier to maintain and test.

5. Use Comments Wisely

Comments should explain "why" something is done, especially when the logic is complex or non-obvious. Over-commenting trivial code can clutter the code and make it harder to maintain. Comments should be used sparingly and meaningfully.

Guidelines:

- Write clear comments when the intent behind a block of code isn't obvious.
- Avoid commenting every line, especially for simple operations.

Example:
```
// Good practice
const TAX_RATE = 0.07; // Tax rate for the state of California

function calculateTotalPrice(price) {
    let tax = price * TAX_RATE;
    return price + tax;
}
```

Explanation:

- The comment clarifies that the TAX_RATE constant represents the tax rate for a specific region.
- The code itself is simple, so no additional comments are needed.

---

6. Avoid Nested Loops and Deep Nesting

Excessive nesting can quickly make code unreadable and hard to maintain. Refactor deeply nested code into separate functions or simplify the logic.

Guidelines:

- Try to keep the nesting level to a minimum.
- If a function is too nested, consider breaking it up into smaller, more manageable functions.

Example:
```
// Bad practice
for (let i = 0; i < orders.length; i++) {
    for (let j = 0; j < orders[i].items.length; j++) {
        if (orders[i].items[j].status === 'pending') {
            // Do something
        }
    }
}

// Good practice
function checkPendingItems(order) {
```

```
        return order.items.filter(item => item.status === 'pending');
}

for (let i = 0; i < orders.length; i++) {
    let pendingItems = checkPendingItems(orders[i]);
    if (pendingItems.length > 0) {
        // Do something
    }
}
```

Explanation:

- In the "Bad practice" example, the double for-loop and the `if` condition create deep nesting, which makes the logic harder to follow.
- The "Good practice" example refactors the inner loop into a separate function, making the code cleaner and more readable.

.

Debugging JavaScript

Debugging is an essential part of the software development process. It involves identifying, diagnosing, and fixing issues in your code. JavaScript, being a client-side language, offers a variety of tools and methods to help developers debug their code effectively. Debugging can be as simple as using `console.log()` or as advanced as stepping through the code with breakpoints in browser developer tools. Below are the most common methods for debugging JavaScript.

1. Using `console.log()` for Debugging

One of the simplest and most common methods for debugging is using the `console.log()` function. This allows developers to print values to the console at various points in the code, making it easier to check variable states and trace the flow of execution.

How to Use:

- You can log any variable or value in JavaScript to understand what's happening at a certain point in the code.
- It is often used to monitor variable values, track function calls, and debug complex expressions.

Example:
```
let price = 100;
let discount = 0.2;

console.log("Price:", price); // Check the initial price
```

```
console.log("Discount:", discount); // Check the discount
let finalPrice = price - (price * discount);
console.log("Final Price:", finalPrice); // Check the final price
```

Explanation:

- In this example, `console.log()` is used to print out the values of `price`, `discount`, and `finalPrice` at different points in the program.
- It helps track the flow of the code and identify if the values are what you expect them to be.

---

2. Using Breakpoints in Developer Tools

Modern browsers (such as Chrome, Firefox, etc.) come with built-in developer tools that provide advanced debugging features. One of the most powerful tools is **setting breakpoints**. This allows you to pause the execution of your JavaScript code at a specific line and inspect the values of variables, the call stack, and more.

How to Use:

1. Open the browser's developer tools (press `F12` or `Ctrl+Shift+I` in Chrome).
2. Go to the "Sources" tab, which displays the code in the current page.
3. Click on the line number where you want to set a breakpoint.
4. When the execution reaches that point, the script will pause, and you can inspect variables and step through the code.

Example:

- Suppose you are debugging a function that calculates a discount:

```
function calculateDiscount(price, discount) {
    let finalPrice = price - (price * discount);
    return finalPrice;
}
calculateDiscount(100, 0.2);
```

- To debug:
  - Set a breakpoint on the `let finalPrice = price - (price * discount);` line.
  - When the code reaches this line, it will pause, and you can inspect the values of `price` and `discount` to ensure they are correct.
  - You can also step through the code to see how the program continues execution.

---

3. Using `debugger` Statement

The `debugger` statement is a built-in JavaScript feature that allows you to pause execution and bring up the browser's developer tools, just like setting a breakpoint manually.

How to Use:

- Insert the `debugger;` statement at any point in your code where you want to halt execution and begin debugging.
- The browser will stop executing at the `debugger` statement and allow you to inspect the current state in the developer tools.

Example:
```
function calculateDiscount(price, discount) {
    debugger; // Execution will pause here
    let finalPrice = price - (price * discount);
    return finalPrice;
}

calculateDiscount(100, 0.2);
```

Explanation:

- In this example, when the `debugger;` statement is encountered, the browser will pause the execution of the code and open the developer tools at the breakpoint.
- You can then inspect the variables `price`, `discount`, and `finalPrice` directly in the console.

---

4. Using `try...catch` for Error Handling

Errors are a common occurrence in JavaScript, especially when dealing with asynchronous code or unpredictable input. The `try...catch` statement allows you to handle runtime errors gracefully and prevent your program from crashing.

How to Use:

- Enclose the potentially error-prone code within a `try` block.
- If an error occurs, it will be caught by the `catch` block, and you can handle it (e.g., log it or show an error message).
- This is especially useful for catching runtime errors and preventing crashes in production code.

Example:
```
try {
    let result = riskyFunction(); // This function might throw an error
} catch (error) {
    console.error("Error occurred:", error); // Log the error to the console
}
```

Explanation:

- The `try` block contains the code that might throw an error, in this case, the `riskyFunction()`.
- If an error occurs, it is caught in the `catch` block, where it can be logged or handled accordingly. This prevents the entire program from failing due to an error in one function.

---

5. Using Linting Tools (ESLint)

Linting tools like **ESLint** are used to automatically check your JavaScript code for potential issues, style violations, and best practices. These tools analyze your code statically (without running it) to find possible errors and enforce coding standards.

How to Use:

- Install and configure a linter like ESLint in your project.
- The linter will check your code against a set of rules and provide feedback on areas that need improvement.

Example:

1. **Install ESLint** (if using Node.js):

   ```
   npm install eslint --save-dev
   ```

2. **Create an ESLint configuration**:

   ```
   npx eslint --init
   ```

3. **Run ESLint**:

   ```
   npx eslint yourFile.js
   ```

4. **Sample Linter Output:**

   ```
   /yourFile.js
   3:10  error  Missing semicolon  semi
   5:2   warning  'let' is not defined  no-undef
   ```

Explanation:

- ESLint will analyze your code and output any errors or warnings.
- It will flag common mistakes such as missing semicolons, undefined variables, or improper code formatting.

Performance Optimization Tips

Performance optimization is crucial for building fast, responsive, and smooth web applications. When JavaScript code runs inefficiently, it can lead to slow load times, unresponsiveness, and poor user experiences. Optimizing your code helps you reduce processing time, avoid unnecessary reflows or repaints, and make your application scale better as it grows.

Here are several key performance optimization tips with practical examples:

---

1. Minimize DOM Manipulations

DOM manipulations are expensive in terms of performance because each change can trigger a reflow (recalculation of layout) and repaint (visual update), especially when done repeatedly. Minimizing these operations can improve the overall performance of your web page.

How to Optimize:

- Instead of making changes to the DOM in a loop, collect the changes first, then apply them all at once.
- Use `document.createDocumentFragment()` to group DOM updates together, so the browser only renders the final result.

Bad Practice:
```
// Modifying DOM multiple times (inefficient)
for (let i = 0; i < items.length; i++) {
    document.body.appendChild(items[i]);
}
```
Good Practice:
```javascript
Copy code
// Modifying DOM only once (efficient)
let fragment = document.createDocumentFragment();
for (let i = 0; i < items.length; i++) {
    fragment.appendChild(items[i]);
}
document.body.appendChild(fragment);  // Only one DOM update
```

Explanation:

- In the bad practice example, the DOM is modified multiple times, which could cause multiple reflows/repaints.
- In the good practice example, a `DocumentFragment` is used to accumulate changes in memory. Only after all changes are made is the DOM updated, which is more efficient.

---

2. Debouncing and Throttling for Events

Certain events, such as `scroll`, `resize`, and `keydown`, can fire many times within a short period, which may lead to performance issues if their associated functions are executed repeatedly. **Debouncing** and **throttling** are techniques to limit the number of function executions in such cases.

Debouncing:

Debouncing ensures that a function is only called after a certain amount of idle time. This is useful for events like window resizing or keypresses where you want to wait until the user stops interacting before executing the function.

Example (Debouncing for Resize Event):
```
let timeout;
function handleResize() {
    clearTimeout(timeout);  // Clear any previous timeouts
    timeout = setTimeout(() => {
        console.log("Resized");  // Execute function after a delay
    }, 200);  // 200ms delay
}

window.addEventListener("resize", handleResize);
```

Explanation:

- The `setTimeout` inside the `handleResize` function delays execution until the user stops resizing the window for 200 milliseconds.
- The `clearTimeout` ensures that only the last resize event triggers the function.

Throttling:

Throttling ensures that a function is called at a maximum frequency, regardless of how many times an event fires.

Example (Throttling for Scroll Event):
```
let lastTime = 0;
function handleScroll() {
    let currentTime = new Date().getTime();
    if (currentTime - lastTime >= 100) {  // Limit to once every 100ms
        console.log("Scrolled");
        lastTime = currentTime;
    }
}

window.addEventListener("scroll", handleScroll);
```

Explanation:

- The scroll handler is throttled so that the function is called no more than once every 100 milliseconds, preventing unnecessary calls while scrolling.

---

3. Avoid Memory Leaks

Memory leaks occur when references to unused objects are not properly cleared, leading to memory consumption that grows over time. This can slow down performance, especially in long-running applications.

How to Avoid Memory Leaks:

- Always remove event listeners when they are no longer needed.
- Ensure that any references to DOM elements or objects that are no longer in use are cleaned up.

Example:
```
// Adding an event listener
const button = document.getElementById("myButton");
function onClick() {
    alert("Button clicked");
}
button.addEventListener("click", onClick);

// Removing the event listener when done
button.removeEventListener("click", onClick);
```

Explanation:

- By removing the event listener using `removeEventListener`, you ensure that the memory allocated for it is freed, avoiding a memory leak.

---

4. Lazy Loading Images and Resources

Lazy loading helps optimize the loading of images and other resources that are not immediately needed when the page loads. It defers the loading of these resources until they are needed, typically when they are visible in the viewport. This reduces initial load time and improves the overall performance of the web page.

How to Implement:

- Use the `loading="lazy"` attribute on images to enable lazy loading.
- This can be particularly useful for images in long scrollable pages.

Example:
```
<img src="image.jpg" loading="lazy" alt="Lazy loaded image">
```

Explanation:

- The `loading="lazy"` attribute ensures that the image is only loaded when it is about to enter the viewport, reducing the initial load time and saving bandwidth.

---

5. Use Web Workers for Heavy Computation

JavaScript runs in a single thread, which means heavy computation can block the main thread and cause the user interface to become unresponsive. **Web Workers** allow you to offload heavy computations to separate threads, preventing the UI from freezing.

How to Use Web Workers:

- Web Workers run in the background, allowing you to perform tasks without blocking the main thread.
- You can communicate with the worker using the `postMessage` and `onmessage` methods.

Example (Using Web Workers for Heavy Computation):

1. **worker.js** (Worker Script):

```
self.onmessage = function(event) {
    if (event.data === "startHeavyComputation") {
        let result = heavyComputation();
        postMessage(result);   // Send result back to main thread
    }
};

function heavyComputation() {
    // Simulate a heavy computation task
    let sum = 0;
    for (let i = 0; i < 1000000000; i++) {
        sum += i;
    }
    return sum; }
```

2. **Main Script (HTML/JavaScript):**

```javascript
const worker = new Worker('worker.js');
worker.postMessage("startHeavyComputation");  // Send a message to start the
computation

worker.onmessage = function(event) {
    console.log("Result:", event.data);  // Handle the result from the worker
};
```

Explanation:

- The **worker.js** script contains the heavy computation logic. This code runs in the background without blocking the main thread.
- The main script communicates with the worker, sending a message to start the computation. Once the worker completes the task, it sends the result back, allowing the main thread to continue running smoothly.

25 multiple-choice questions (MCQs) based on the topics "Writing Clean and Readable Code," "Debugging JavaScript," and "Performance Optimization Tips."

Writing Clean and Readable Code

1. **Which of the following is an example of a good variable name in JavaScript?**
   - a) `x`
   - b) `tempValue`
   - c) `finalTotalPrice`
   - d) `a`

   Answer: c) `finalTotalPrice`

2. **What does the term "magic number" refer to in programming?**
   - a) A number that is randomly generated
   - b) A hardcoded number without explanation
   - c) A unique number used for encryption
   - d) A number with special significance in the code

   Answer: b) A hardcoded number without explanation

3. **Which of the following is the preferred indentation style in JavaScript?**
   - a) 1 space
   - b) 2 spaces
   - c) 4 spaces

o   d) Tabs

Answer: b) 2 spaces (or c) 4 spaces, depending on project conventions)

4. **What is the main purpose of using descriptive variable names?**
   o   a) To reduce code length
   o   b) To make the code easier to understand and maintain
   o   c) To confuse the reader
   o   d) To avoid using comments

Answer: b) To make the code easier to understand and maintain

5. **Which of the following is an example of avoiding deep nesting in functions?**
   o   a) Using a large `for` loop
   o   b) Refactoring deeply nested logic into separate functions
   o   c) Using multiple conditional statements
   o   d) Using a single function for all operations

Answer: b) Refactoring deeply nested logic into separate functions

6. **When should you use comments in your code?**
   o   a) To explain simple code
   o   b) To explain the intention behind complex logic
   o   c) To comment out working code
   o   d) To fill space between code blocks

Answer: b) To explain the intention behind complex logic

7. **What is the recommended practice for function length in JavaScript?**
   o   a) Functions should be as short as possible
   o   b) Functions should contain all logic in one block
   o   c) Functions should do one thing and do it well
   o   d) Functions should have as many parameters as possible

Answer: c) Functions should do one thing and do it well

8. **What is the purpose of using `const` for variables that do not change?**
   o   a) To prevent accidental reassignment
   o   b) To make the code more readable
   o   c) To declare variables that will never be used
   o   d) To allocate more memory

Answer: a) To prevent accidental reassignment

9. **What is the consequence of using ambiguous variable names?**
   - o a) It reduces the execution time
   - o b) It makes the code harder to maintain and understand
   - o c) It makes the code easier to optimize
   - o d) It results in a syntax error

   Answer: b) It makes the code harder to maintain and understand

10. **Which of the following should you avoid to make your code more readable?**
    - o a) Writing comments for complex logic
    - o b) Using descriptive names for functions and variables
    - o c) Using one-letter variable names like x or y
    - o d) Breaking code into small, focused functions

    Answer: c) Using one-letter variable names like x or y

Debugging JavaScript

11. **What is the primary purpose of using `console.log()` in JavaScript?**
    - o a) To execute functions
    - o b) To print values and check variable states
    - o c) To test the performance of the code
    - o d) To create new JavaScript objects

    Answer: b) To print values and check variable states

12. **Which browser tool allows you to step through your JavaScript code line by line for debugging?**
    - o a) Chrome DevTools
    - o b) Node.js
    - o c) V8 Engine
    - o d) Sublime Text

    Answer: a) Chrome DevTools

13. **Which keyword in JavaScript can pause code execution and allow inspection of the current state?**
    - o a) `stop()`
    - o b) `breakpoint()`
    - o c) `debugger`
    - o d) `pause`

    Answer: c) `debugger`

14. **What is the purpose of the `try...catch` block in JavaScript?**
    - o a) To catch logical errors
    - o b) To handle runtime errors
    - o c) To stop code execution
    - o d) To print error messages

    Answer: b) To handle runtime errors

15. **What should you use to identify and fix potential problems in your JavaScript code before running it?**
    - o a) Logging to the console
    - o b) Web workers
    - o c) Linting tools like ESLint
    - o d) Dynamic typing

    Answer: c) Linting tools like ESLint

16. **What is the correct way to check if a variable is defined using a `try...catch` block?**
    - o a) `try { variable; } catch (error) { console.log("Error:", error); }`
    - o b) `if (variable === undefined) { console.log("Not defined"); }`
    - o c) `if (typeof variable === "undefined") { console.log("Not defined"); }`
    - o d) Both a and c

    Answer: d) Both a and c

17. **What is a breakpoint in debugging?**
    - o a) A place where the program pauses so you can inspect its state
    - o b) A method to handle errors
    - o c) A function that runs before the program starts
    - o d) A line of code that performs error handling

    Answer: a) A place where the program pauses so you can inspect its state

18. **Which of the following will help to log multiple variables at once?**
    - o a) `console.log(variable1 + variable2)`
    - o b) `console.log([variable1, variable2])`
    - o c) `console.log(variable1); console.log(variable2)`
    - o d) All of the above

    Answer: d) All of the above

19. **What does the `typeof` operator do in JavaScript?**
    - o a) It converts a variable to a specific type
    - o b) It checks the data type of a variable
    - o c) It defines a new variable type
    - o d) It throws a runtime error

Answer: b) It checks the data type of a variable

Performance Optimization Tips

20. **Why is it important to minimize DOM manipulations in JavaScript?**
    - o a) It reduces the number of HTTP requests
    - o b) It avoids layout recalculations and repainting, which can be performance-intensive
    - o c) It reduces memory usage
    - o d) It speeds up JavaScript execution

Answer: b) It avoids layout recalculations and repainting, which can be performance-intensive

21. **What is the purpose of `document.createDocumentFragment()` in DOM manipulation?**
    - o a) It speeds up the rendering of the page by storing changes in memory
    - o b) It creates a new DOM element to be appended
    - o c) It clears the DOM tree
    - o d) It splits the DOM into smaller fragments

Answer: a) It speeds up the rendering of the page by storing changes in memory

22. **Which of the following techniques limits the number of times an event handler is executed?**
    - o a) Throttling
    - o b) Debouncing
    - o c) Both throttling and debouncing
    - o d) Event delegation

Answer: c) Both throttling and debouncing

23. **What does debouncing do for a resize or scroll event?**
    - o a) It executes the function after a fixed number of events
    - o b) It limits the number of function calls by grouping multiple calls together
    - o c) It only calls the function when the event ends
    - o d) It ensures the function is executed continuously while the event is firing

Answer: c) It only calls the function when the event ends

24. **Why should you remove event listeners when they are no longer needed?**
    - o a) To prevent memory leaks and improve performance
    - o b) To free up space in the DOM
    - o c) To reduce page load times
    - o d) To ensure the event is triggered only once

    Answer: a) To prevent memory leaks and improve performance

25. **What is lazy loading in the context of web performance?**
    - o a) Loading all images immediately when the page loads
    - o b) Delaying the loading of resources like images until they are needed
    - o c) Using cached data to speed up the page load
    - o d) Compressing images to reduce load time

    Answer: b) Delaying the loading of resources like images until they are needed

CHAPTER-9

JAVASCRIPT FRAMEWORKS AND LIBRARIES

1. Introduction to Popular Frameworks (React, Angular, Vue)

JavaScript frameworks are powerful tools that simplify the process of building complex web applications. These frameworks offer built-in structures, libraries, and tools that reduce the time developers spend on routine tasks like DOM manipulation, state management, and routing. Some of the most widely used JavaScript frameworks include **React**, **Angular**, and **Vue.js**. Let's take a detailed look at each of these frameworks.

1.1 React

React is a popular JavaScript library, developed by Facebook, for building user interfaces (UIs) in a component-based architecture. React focuses on creating reusable, interactive components that handle their own state.

Key Features of React:

- **Component-Based Architecture**: React divides the UI into smaller, reusable components. Each component is responsible for rendering part of the UI and handling its own state.
- **JSX Syntax**: React uses **JSX** (JavaScript XML), an extension that allows developers to write HTML-like code directly in JavaScript. JSX is not required, but it makes the code easier to read and maintain.
- **Virtual DOM**: React uses a Virtual DOM (VDOM), which is a lightweight copy of the real DOM. React updates the VDOM first, compares it with the real DOM, and only applies changes where necessary, making the application faster.
- **State and Props**: React components can store and manage data through **state**. **Props** are used to pass data between components. This unidirectional data flow is key to React's design.

Example: React Component:

```
import React, { useState } from 'react';

function Counter() {
  const [count, setCount] = useState(0);

  return (
    <div>
      <p>You clicked {count} times</p>
      <button onClick={() => setCount(count + 1)}>Click me</button>
    </div>
  );
}

export default Counter;
```

Explanation:

- The `useState` hook is used to create a piece of state (count) and a method (`setCount`) to update that state.
- When the button is clicked, `setCount(count + 1)` is called, updating the count, and React re-renders the component.
- This example demonstrates React's declarative UI model, where you declare what the UI should look like based on the current state.

1.2 Angular

Angular is a robust, full-featured framework developed by Google. It is ideal for building large-scale, enterprise-grade applications. Unlike React, Angular is a **complete framework** that includes everything you need to build sophisticated apps, from routing to state management.

Key Features of Angular:

- **TypeScript-Based**: Angular is built using TypeScript, a superset of JavaScript. TypeScript adds strong typing, making code easier to understand, debug, and maintain.
- **Two-Way Data Binding**: Angular's **two-way data binding** allows changes in the application's model (data) to be reflected in the view (UI) and vice versa. This feature helps to synchronize the view and data without manual intervention.
- **Dependency Injection**: Angular has a powerful **dependency injection** system that allows components to access services (such as HTTP services) without directly creating instances.
- **Directives and Services**: Angular uses **directives** to extend HTML functionality and **services** to encapsulate business logic and interact with back-end APIs.

Example: Angular Component:
```
import { Component } from '@angular/core';

@Component({
  selector: 'app-counter',
  template: `
    <div>
      <p>You clicked {{ count }} times</p>
      <button (click)="increment()">Click me</button>
    </div>
  `
})
export class CounterComponent {
  count: number = 0;

  increment() {
    this.count++;
  }
}
```

Explanation:

- The {{ count }} syntax is Angular's way of binding data to the view (HTML).
- The (click) event binding listens for the click event and calls the increment() method when the button is clicked.
- Angular uses TypeScript for static typing and class-based components, making the code more predictable and easier to debug.

1.3 Vue.js

Vue.js is a progressive framework designed for building user interfaces. It is called "progressive" because you can adopt it incrementally — start with a simple component and gradually move toward building more complex applications. Vue is often praised for its simplicity and ease of integration.

Key Features of Vue:

- **Declarative Rendering**: Vue's **declarative rendering** syntax allows you to bind data directly to the DOM with an intuitive, easy-to-understand syntax.
- **Single-File Components**: Vue allows developers to define the HTML, JavaScript, and CSS of a component in a single .vue file, leading to cleaner and more organized code.
- **Reactivity System**: Vue's reactivity system ensures that when data changes, the DOM is automatically updated to reflect those changes.
- **Vue Router and Vuex**: Vue provides **Vue Router** for handling navigation and **Vuex** for centralized state management, making it easier to manage large applications.

Example: Vue.js Component:

```
<div id="app">
  <p>You clicked {{ count }} times</p>
  <button @click="increment">Click me</button>
</div>

<script>
  new Vue({
    el: '#app',
    data: {
      count: 0
    },
    methods: {
      increment() {
        this.count++;
      }
    }
  });
</script>
```

Explanation:

- The `{{ count }}` syntax binds the `count` data property to the view.
- The `@click` directive is shorthand for the `v-on:click` directive and binds the `increment()` method to the button's click event.
- This example shows how Vue's simple and intuitive syntax allows for quick UI updates without much boilerplate code.

Comparison of React, Angular, and Vue

Feature	React	Angular	Vue
Type	Library	Full Framework	Progressive Framework
Core Language	JavaScript (JSX)	TypeScript	JavaScript
Data Binding	One-way (via Props/State)	Two-way Data Binding	One-way (via data and props)
State Management	React Context, Redux, Zustand	RxJS, NgRx	Vuex (official state management)
Routing	React Router	Angular Router	Vue Router
Learning Curve	Moderate	Steep (full framework with TypeScript)	Easy to Moderate
Community and Ecosystem	Very Large	Large	Growing but smaller than React/Angular
Performance	High (with Virtual DOM)	High (with change detection)	High (with reactivity system)

2. Using JavaScript Libraries (jQuery, Lodash)

JavaScript libraries are collections of pre-written code that developers can use to perform common tasks more efficiently. These libraries focus on specific aspects of development and help reduce the amount of code you need to write from scratch. Two widely used libraries are **jQuery** and **Lodash**. Let's dive deeper into each of these libraries, their features, and practical examples.

2.1 jQuery

jQuery is a fast, lightweight, and feature-rich JavaScript library that simplifies common tasks like DOM manipulation, event handling, and AJAX calls. Although it has become less prominent with the advent of modern JavaScript frameworks like React and Angular, jQuery is still widely used in many existing web applications and simpler projects due to its simplicity and ease of use.

Key Features of jQuery:

1. **DOM Manipulation**: jQuery provides an easy-to-use syntax for selecting and modifying DOM elements, which helps avoid the complexity of native JavaScript.
2. **Event Handling**: jQuery offers simple methods for attaching event listeners, such as clicks, hover, and key presses. It normalizes cross-browser differences.
3. **AJAX (Asynchronous JavaScript and XML)**: jQuery simplifies making asynchronous HTTP requests, allowing you to send and receive data from a server without reloading the page.

Example: jQuery for Event Handling and DOM Manipulation

```html
<!DOCTYPE html>
<html>
<head>
  <script src="https://code.jquery.com/jquery-3.6.0.min.js"></script>
</head>
<body>
  <button id="myButton">Click Me</button>
  <div id="message"></div>

  <script>
    // jQuery click event handler
    $('#myButton').click(function() {
      // Update the text content of the #message div
      $('#message').text('Button clicked!');
    });
  </script>
</body>
</html>
```

Explanation:

- In this example, jQuery's $ function is used to select the button element with the ID `#myButton`.
- The `click()` method is then attached to the button, so when it is clicked, the text of the `#message` div is changed to "Button clicked!" using `text()` method.
- jQuery simplifies this process by abstracting away complex DOM manipulation code and cross-browser compatibility issues.

2.2 Lodash

Lodash is a modern, highly optimized utility library that provides a wide range of helper functions for working with arrays, objects, and functions. Lodash is particularly helpful for performing common operations like array manipulation, deep cloning, debouncing, and throttling. It aims to simplify JavaScript development and improve code readability and performance.

Key Features of Lodash:

1. **Array Manipulation**: Lodash provides methods like `map`, `filter`, `reduce`, `find`, etc., that simplify and optimize operations on arrays.
2. **Object Manipulation**: Lodash has several utilities for objects, including deep cloning (`cloneDeep`), checking properties (`has`), merging objects (`merge`), and more.
3. **Utility Functions**: Lodash also includes methods like `debounce`, `throttle`, and `memoize` that are helpful for performance optimization in specific use cases, such as limiting the frequency of function calls or caching results.

Example: Lodash for Deep Cloning an Object

```
// Lodash example for deep cloning an object
const _ = require('lodash');

const object1 = { a: 1, b: { c: 2 } };
const object2 = _.cloneDeep(object1);

object2.b.c = 3;

console.log(object1.b.c); // Output: 2
console.log(object2.b.c); // Output: 3
```

Explanation:

- In this example, Lodash's `_.cloneDeep` method is used to create a deep copy of the `object1`.
- When we modify the `b.c` property of `object2`, the change does not affect `object1`, because Lodash ensures that the cloned object is independent of the original object.
- `_.cloneDeep` is useful when you need to avoid unintended side effects from mutating objects or arrays in your code.

Comparison of jQuery and Lodash

While **jQuery** and **Lodash** can be used together in a project, they serve different purposes:

Feature	jQuery	Lodash
Purpose	Simplifies DOM manipulation and events	Provides utility functions for arrays, objects, and functions
DOM Manipulation	Yes	No
Event Handling	Yes	No
AJAX Support	Yes	No
Array Manipulation	Basic operations with arrays	Advanced methods like `map`, `filter`, `reduce`
Object Manipulation	No	Methods like `cloneDeep`, `merge`, `has`
Performance Optimization	No	Methods like `debounce`, `throttle`, `memoize`
Use Case	Enhancing UI, event handling, AJAX	Optimizing and simplifying data manipulation tasks

Summary:

- **React** focuses on building reusable components, offering a rich ecosystem and strong performance optimizations.
- **Angular** is a comprehensive framework that supports large-scale applications, with two-way data binding and dependency injection.
- **Vue.js** provides a lightweight, flexible solution with easy-to-understand features like reactive data binding and single-file components.
- **jQuery** simplifies DOM manipulation and AJAX handling but is becoming less common in modern web development.
- **Lodash** is a utility library that simplifies common JavaScript tasks like array manipulation, deep cloning, and function debouncing.

Each framework and library is designed for specific use cases, and the choice depends on the complexity of the application, developer preferences, and the project's requirements.

25 multiple-choice questions (MCQs) on the topics **Introduction to Popular Frameworks (React, Angular, Vue)** and **Using JavaScript Libraries (jQuery, Lodash):**

Introduction to Popular Frameworks (React, Angular, Vue)

1. **Which of the following is the primary language used in Angular?**
   - o A) JavaScript
   - o B) TypeScript
   - o C) Java
   - o D) Python

   Answer: B) TypeScript

2. **What is the main advantage of using React's Virtual DOM?**
   - o A) It reduces the amount of code needed.
   - o B) It optimizes rendering by reducing direct DOM manipulation.
   - o C) It adds more features to the DOM.
   - o D) It allows better styling of components.

   Answer: B) It optimizes rendering by reducing direct DOM manipulation.

3. **Which method in React is used to manage the state of a component?**
   - o A) useRef
   - o B) useState
   - o C) useContext
   - o D) useEffect

   Answer: B) useState

4. **Which of the following is a key feature of Angular's two-way data binding?**
   - o A) Changes to the view automatically update the model.
   - o B) Changes to the model automatically update the view.
   - o C) Both model and view update only when the component reloads.
   - o D) No data binding occurs.

   Answer: B) Changes to the model automatically update the view.

5. **Which directive is used to define a component's template in Angular?**
   - o A) @NgModule
   - o B) @Component
   - o C) @ViewChild
   - o D) @Input

   Answer: B) @Component

6. **In Vue.js, how are components registered?**
   - o A) In the main.js file
   - o B) By using the Vue.component method
   - o C) Through Vuex store
   - o D) Automatically through the template

   Answer: B) By using the Vue.component method

7. **Which of the following Vue.js directives is used for event handling?**
   - o A) v-if
   - o B) v-for
   - o C) v-bind
   - o D) v-on

   Answer: D) v-on

8. **Which feature in React allows you to create reusable UI components?**
   - o A) Virtual DOM
   - o B) Functional components
   - o C) Hooks
   - o D) JSX

   Answer: B) Functional components

9. **What is the purpose of the `ngOnInit()` method in Angular?**
   - o A) To initialize the data in the component.
   - o B) To destroy the component.
   - o C) To handle HTTP requests.
   - o D) To set up two-way data binding.

   Answer: A) To initialize the data in the component.

10. **In Vue.js, which method is used to modify reactive data?**
    - o A) v-bind
    - o B) data()
    - o C) methods()
    - o D) set()

    Answer: B) data()

11. **Which statement about React's JSX is true?**
    - o A) JSX is a programming language.
    - o B) JSX allows HTML to be written directly in JavaScript code.
    - o C) JSX is only used for CSS styling.
    - o D) JSX is a JavaScript extension for routing.

Answer: B) JSX allows HTML to be written directly in JavaScript code.

12. **In Angular, which of the following handles the HTTP requests and responses?**
    - o A) ngRoute
    - o B) Angular CLI
    - o C) HttpClientModule
    - o D) ngModule

    Answer: C) HttpClientModule

13. **What is the purpose of Vuex in Vue.js?**
    - o A) To handle events in the components
    - o B) For managing state in the application
    - o C) To create reusable components
    - o D) To bind data between views

    Answer: B) For managing state in the application

14. **Which of the following is not a feature of React?**
    - o A) Component-based architecture
    - o B) One-way data binding
    - o C) TypeScript support
    - o D) Direct DOM manipulation

    Answer: D) Direct DOM manipulation

15. **Which of the following is used to bind data to the template in Angular?**
    - o A) v-model
    - o B) ngModel
    - o C) {{ variable }}
    - o D) {{ state }}

    Answer: B) ngModel

Using JavaScript Libraries (jQuery, Lodash)

16. **Which of the following is a primary feature of jQuery?**
    - o A) DOM manipulation and event handling
    - o B) Dependency injection
    - o C) State management
    - o D) Data binding

    Answer: A) DOM manipulation and event handling

17. **In jQuery, which function is used to hide an element?**
    - o A) hide()
    - o B) disappear()
    - o C) remove()
    - o D) collapse()

    Answer: A) hide()

18. **Which method in Lodash is used to create a deep copy of an object?**
    - o A) _.clone
    - o B) _.merge
    - o C) _.cloneDeep
    - o D) _.deepCopy

    Answer: C) _.cloneDeep

19. **Which of the following is a method provided by Lodash for iterating over collections?**
    - o A) _.map
    - o B) _.bind
    - o C) _.each
    - o D) Both A and C

    Answer: D) Both A and C

20. **Which of the following jQuery functions is used to perform an AJAX request?**
    - o A) $.ajax()
    - o B) $.request()
    - o C) $.http()
    - o D) $.call()

    Answer: A) $.ajax()

21. **Which function in jQuery is used to set or get the value of form elements?**
    - o A) .input()
    - o B) .value()
    - o C) .val()
    - o D) .setValue()

    Answer: C) .val()

22. **Which of the following functions in Lodash is used to delay the invocation of a function?**
    - o A) _.delay
    - o B) _.debounce
    - o C) _.throttle

o   D) All of the above

Answer: D) All of the above

23. **What is the main advantage of using `$.get()` in jQuery?**
    o   A) It binds DOM elements.
    o   B) It retrieves JSON data from a server.
    o   C) It manipulates events.
    o   D) It performs mathematical operations.

    Answer: B) It retrieves JSON data from a server.

24. **What does the `_.debounce` function in Lodash do?**
    o   A) It prevents a function from being called too frequently.
    o   B) It triggers a function immediately after it is called.
    o   C) It limits function execution to a specific interval.
    o   D) It repeats function calls until a condition is met.

    Answer: A) It prevents a function from being called too frequently.

25. **Which jQuery method is used to append content to the selected element?**
    o   A) .append()
    o   B) .prepend()
    o   C) .add()
    o   D) .inject()

    Answer: A) .append()

CHAPTER-10

FINAL PROJECT: BUILDING A WEB APPLICATION

1. Planning and Designing the Application

Planning and designing an application is a critical first step in the development process. It involves determining the application's purpose, the features it will include, the user experience (UX), and how the code will be structured. A well-planned application is more maintainable, scalable, and user-friendly.

Steps to Plan and Design an Application:

1. **Define the Purpose and Requirements**:
   o **Identify the Problem**: What problem does your application solve? It could be something like improving workflow, offering a service, or providing entertainment.
   o **User Stories**: Gather user stories or feature requests. What do users expect from the app? This could include login functionality, data manipulation, etc.
   o **Functional vs. Non-Functional Requirements**: Functional requirements describe specific behaviors (like login or data submission), while non-functional ones describe system performance (like speed, scalability, and security).

2. **Wireframing and UI/UX Design**:
   o **Wireframes**: A wireframe is a low-fidelity mock-up of the app, usually a simple visual representation of the layout. Tools like **Figma**, **Sketch**, or **Adobe XD** are often used for this purpose.
   o **UI Design**: After wireframes, the next step is creating detailed UI designs, including colors, typography, buttons, forms, and other elements. The design should ensure it's intuitive, easy to navigate, and responsive.
   o **User Flow**: Plan how the user will navigate through the application. For example, after a user logs in, they should be directed to a dashboard.

3. **Define the Technology Stack**:
   o **Frontend Technologies**: Based on the app's design, you'll choose the appropriate frontend technologies like **React**, **Angular**, or **Vue.js**.
   o **Backend Technologies**: Decide whether the app needs a server-side language like **Node.js**, **Django**, or **Ruby on Rails**.
   o **Databases**: Choose between relational databases (like **MySQL** or **PostgreSQL**) or NoSQL databases (like **MongoDB**).
   o **APIs**: Identify the external services you'll need (e.g., payment processing, geolocation APIs) and how they will be integrated.

4. **Structure and Break Down Features**:
   o **Modularization**: Break the application into smaller, manageable features or components. For instance, in a to-do app, you might have components like "Task List," "Add Task," and "Task Manager."
   o **Database Schema**: Design the database schema and identify the relationships between entities. For example, you may have a `User` table and a `Tasks` table, with a one-to-many relationship.

5. **Define a Project Timeline**:
   - o **Agile Development**: Often, development is broken down into sprints (typically 2 weeks). Define the tasks to be completed in each sprint, starting with essential features.
   - o **Milestones**: Set key milestones for each feature's completion, such as a working prototype or MVP (Minimum Viable Product).

2. Writing JavaScript for Interactive Features

JavaScript is the backbone of interactivity on web pages, allowing developers to create dynamic and responsive user interfaces. Through JavaScript, you can respond to user input, manipulate the document structure, fetch data from a server, animate elements, validate forms, and more. Let's explore some key concepts to implement interactive features in JavaScript:

1. Event Handling

Event handling in JavaScript refers to responding to user actions, such as clicks, form submissions, or keyboard presses. By using event listeners, you can trigger specific functions or actions when an event occurs.

How it works:

- **Event Listeners**: These are functions that wait for specific events (like click or keypress) to occur and then run the code specified inside them.

Example: Handling a Button Click to Display a Message
```
const button = document.getElementById('myButton');
button.addEventListener('click', function() {
    alert('Button clicked!');
});
```

In this example:

- When the user clicks the button, the event listener listens for the `click` event.
- Once triggered, it executes the function inside, which displays a message (`alert`).

You can also remove event listeners dynamically using `removeEventListener()` if needed.

2. DOM Manipulation

The DOM (Document Object Model) represents the structure of your HTML page, and JavaScript allows you to modify it dynamically. This can involve changing the content, styles, or structure of elements in response to user interactions.

How it works:

- **DOM Methods:** Methods like `getElementById()`, `querySelector()`, `textContent`, `innerHTML`, and others are used to manipulate HTML elements.
- **Style Manipulation:** You can also modify CSS properties using JavaScript.

Example: Dynamically Changing the Text Content of a Paragraph
```
const paragraph = document.getElementById('myParagraph');
paragraph.textContent = 'New text content!';
```

In this example:

- The `getElementById()` method selects the paragraph element with the ID `myParagraph`.
- The `textContent` property is then changed to `'New text content!'`, which updates the paragraph text.

Similarly, you can modify other properties like `innerHTML`, `style`, etc., to change the content or appearance.

---

3. AJAX and Fetch API for Data Fetching

AJAX (Asynchronous JavaScript and XML) allows you to send or receive data asynchronously from a server without refreshing the page. The `Fetch API` is a modern replacement for older AJAX methods, providing a simpler and more flexible way to make HTTP requests.

How it works:

- You can make asynchronous requests to a server to fetch or send data, and then use JavaScript to update the UI dynamically based on the response.

Example: Fetching User Data from a Server and Displaying It
```
fetch('https://jsonplaceholder.typicode.com/users')
    .then(response => response.json())  // Parse the JSON response
    .then(data => {
        console.log(data);
        document.getElementById('userList').innerHTML = data.map(user =>
`<li>${user.name}</li>`).join('');
    })
    .catch(error => console.error('Error:', error));
```

In this example:

- `fetch()` sends a GET request to the server at the provided URL.
- The response is parsed as JSON with `.json()`.
- The `data.map()` function generates an unordered list of users, which is then inserted into the HTML element with ID `userList`.

AJAX and Fetch allow you to create applications that don't require full-page reloads, making the experience faster and more responsive.

---

4. Animations and Transitions

Animations can enhance user experience by making interfaces more interactive and visually appealing. JavaScript can be used to create smooth animations, either by manipulating CSS properties directly or using the `requestAnimationFrame()` method for better performance.

How it works:

- **CSS Transitions**: You can trigger CSS transitions using JavaScript, allowing elements to change smoothly from one state to another.
- **`requestAnimationFrame()`**: This method schedules an animation to run at the next available browser repaint, providing smoother animations.

Example: Animating a Div Element to Move Horizontally
```
const div = document.getElementById('myDiv');
let pos = 0;

function move() {
    if (pos < 200) {
        pos++;
        div.style.left = pos + 'px';   // Move the div horizontally
        requestAnimationFrame(move);   // Continue the animation
    }
}

move();
```

In this example:

- The `move()` function is repeatedly called by `requestAnimationFrame()`, updating the `left` CSS property of the div.
- The `div` element will gradually move to the right, making the animation smooth and visually appealing.

Animations can be used for transitions between different views, highlighting certain elements, or creating interactive components like sliders.

5. Form Validation

Form validation ensures that the data users enter is correct and meets specific criteria before submission. JavaScript allows you to perform client-side validation to prevent invalid data from being sent to the server.

How it works:

- JavaScript validates the input data when a user submits a form.
- If the validation fails, JavaScript can prevent form submission and display error messages to guide the user.

Example: Checking if a User Has Entered a Valid Email Address

```
const form = document.getElementById('myForm');
form.addEventListener('submit', function(event) {
    const email = document.getElementById('email').value;
    const emailPattern = /^[a-zA-Z0-9._-]+@[a-zA-Z0-9.-]+\.[a-zA-Z]{2,4}$/;

    if (!emailPattern.test(email)) {
        alert('Invalid email address!');
        event.preventDefault();  // Prevent form submission
    }
});
```

In this example:

- A regular expression (`emailPattern`) is used to check if the email input is in a valid format.
- If the email doesn't match the pattern, the form submission is prevented using `event.preventDefault()`, and an alert is shown.

JavaScript validation is essential for improving the user experience and ensuring data integrity.

---

6. Working with APIs

Working with APIs allows you to fetch data, send data, or integrate external services into your application. JavaScript makes it easy to interact with APIs using methods like **fetch()**, which enables asynchronous requests to interact with back-end servers or third-party services.

How it works:

- You can use the `fetch()` API or older methods like `XMLHttpRequest` to interact with APIs.
- Data returned by APIs can be used to update the page dynamically.

Example: Fetching Data from an API

```
const apiUrl = 'https://api.example.com/data';
```

```
async function fetchData() {
    const response = await fetch(apiUrl);
    const data = await response.json();
    console.log(data);
}

fetchData();
```

In this example:

- The `fetchData()` function uses `fetch()` to send a request to an API.
- The `await` keyword is used to pause the function execution until the response is received and parsed into JSON.
- The fetched data is logged to the console.

API interactions can include user authentication, retrieving real-time data, posting data to the server, or integrating third-party services (like social media sharing).

3. Debugging and Testing the Application

Debugging and testing are essential practices in software development to ensure that the application behaves as expected, is free of errors, and delivers a smooth user experience. Debugging helps identify and fix issues, while testing ensures the application works correctly. Here's a detailed explanation of how to debug and test your JavaScript applications effectively.

1. Debugging Techniques

1.1 Using Console Logs

The most common debugging technique is using `console.log()`, which allows you to print out variable values, the flow of execution, and other useful information to understand the current state of your application.

Example:
```
const sum = (a, b) => {
    console.log('a:', a, 'b:', b); // Debugging log
    return a + b;
};

sum(5, 3);
```

- The `console.log()` statement helps print the values of a and b to the console, allowing you to see if the function is receiving the expected inputs and performing as intended.

When to use:

- To inspect variables and their values.
- To trace the flow of execution.
- To check if certain parts of code are being executed.

1.2 Breakpoints and Developer Tools

Modern browsers, such as Chrome, have built-in developer tools that allow you to set **breakpoints** in your JavaScript code. This lets you pause the code execution at specific points and inspect the state of your variables, step through the code, and identify problems.

How to Use Breakpoints in Chrome DevTools:

1. Open DevTools: Press `F12` or `Ctrl + Shift + I` in Chrome.
2. Go to the "Sources" tab.
3. Find your JavaScript file on the left panel.
4. Click the line number to set a breakpoint.
5. Use the "Step Over", "Step Into", and "Step Out" buttons to navigate through the code line by line.

When to use:

- To pause execution at specific points and inspect variables.
- To step through code and see how values change as the code executes.

1.3 Error Handling with try-catch

The `try...catch` block is used to catch and handle errors that may occur during runtime. It allows you to define a code block (`try`) that may throw an error, and a separate block (`catch`) that will run if an error occurs.

Example:
```
try {
    const result = riskyFunction();
} catch (error) {
    console.error('An error occurred:', error);
}
```

- The `riskyFunction()` is called inside the `try` block. If it throws an error, the `catch` block will catch it, preventing the application from crashing and allowing you to log or handle the error.

When to use:

- To handle potential runtime errors and prevent the application from breaking.
- To catch specific errors (e.g., API failures) and log or notify the user.

1.4 Using the debugger Statement

The `debugger` statement is used to pause the execution of the JavaScript code at a specific point and allows you to inspect variables, call stacks, and more in the browser's developer tools.

Example:
```
function calculateTotal(price, discount) {
    debugger; // Execution will pause here
    return price - (price * discount);
}
```

- When the JavaScript engine encounters the `debugger` statement, it will pause execution, and you can inspect the current values of the variables `price` and `discount` in DevTools.

When to use:

- When you want to pause the execution of code and manually inspect the state of variables, call stack, or object properties.
- Useful for inspecting critical sections of the code during execution.

---

2. Testing the Application

Testing ensures the correctness and reliability of the application. There are various levels of testing to ensure different aspects of your application work as expected.

2.1 Unit Testing

Unit testing involves testing individual functions or components in isolation to ensure they behave as expected. Unit tests are typically automated and are essential for validating small units of code (like functions or methods).

Example with Jest (JavaScript Testing Framework):
```
test('adds 1 + 2 to equal 3', () => {
    expect(sum(1, 2)).toBe(3);
});
```

- The `test()` function defines a test case.
- `expect()` defines the expected outcome, and `.toBe()` is a matcher that compares the result of the `sum(1, 2)` to 3.

When to use:

- To test individual functions or methods to ensure they work correctly in isolation.
- Automated tests help ensure that small code changes don't break existing functionality.

2.2 Integration Testing

Integration testing checks if multiple components or modules of the application work together correctly. It ensures that different parts of the application interact properly and that data flows correctly between them.

Example:

- Testing if the user registration process works end-to-end. This might involve testing if the registration form data is correctly validated, sent to the server, and results in a successful user account creation.

When to use:

- To verify that different parts of the application (e.g., front-end and back-end) work together as expected.
- To ensure that integrations with external systems (e.g., APIs) are functioning properly.

2.3 End-to-End (E2E) Testing

End-to-End testing simulates real-world user interactions with the entire application. It ensures that the application functions correctly from start to finish, including user interactions, data flow, and overall user experience.

Example with Cypress (E2E Testing Framework):

```
it('should log in successfully', () => {
    cy.visit('/login');
    cy.get('input[name="username"]').type('testuser');
    cy.get('input[name="password"]').type('password');
    cy.get('button[type="submit"]').click();
    cy.url().should('include', '/dashboard');
});
```

- The `cy.visit()` method navigates to the login page.
- `cy.get()` selects elements on the page (input fields, buttons) and simulates user actions (typing and clicking).

- The test verifies that the URL changes to include /dashboard after a successful login.

When to use:

- To test the application flow from a user's perspective.
- To verify that the application works end-to-end, from data input to the UI update.

2.4 Automated Testing

Automated testing allows tests to be run automatically whenever there are changes in the code. This helps detect errors early in the development process and ensures the application remains stable as it evolves.

Example:

You can set up automated tests using testing frameworks (like Jest, Mocha, or Cypress) and CI/CD (Continuous Integration/Continuous Deployment) pipelines to run tests automatically on every code commit.

When to use:

- To ensure that your application remains bug-free and stable as it changes over time.
- To automatically run tests in a CI/CD pipeline to catch regressions.